AQUINAS
A GUIDE FOR THE PERPLEXED

Continuum *Guides for the Perplexed*

Continuum's Guides for the Perplexed are clear, concise and accessible introductions to thinkers, writers and subjects that students and readers can find especially challenging. Concentrating specifically on what it is that makes the subject difficult to grasp, these books explain and explore key themes and ideas, guiding the reader towards a thorough understanding of demanding material.

Guides for the Perplexed available from Continuum:

Adorno: A Guide for the Perplexed, Alex Thomson
Arendt: A Guide for the Perplexed, Karin Fry
Aristotle: A Guide for the Perplexed, John Vella
Augustine: A Guide for the Perplexed, James Wetzel
Bentham: A Guide for the Perplexed, Philip Schofield
Berkeley: A Guide for the Perplexed, Talia Bettcher
Deleuze: A Guide for the Perplexed, Claire Colebrook
Derrida: A Guide for the Perplexed, Julian Wolfreys
Descartes: A Guide for the Perplexed, Justin Skirry
The Empiricists: A Guide for the Perplexed, Laurence Carlin
Existentialism: A Guide for the Perplexed, Stephen Earnshaw
Freud: A Guide for the Perplexed, Celine Surprenant
Gadamer: A Guide for the Perplexed, Chris Lawn
Habermas: A Guide for the Perplexed, Lasse Thomassen
Hegel: A Guide for the Perplexed, David James
Heidegger: A Guide for the Perplexed, David Cerbone
Hobbes: A Guide for the Perplexed, Stephen J. Finn
Hume: A Guide for the Perplexed, Angela Coventry
Husserl: A Guide for the Perplexed, Matheson Russell
Kant: A Guide for the Perplexed, T. K. Seung
Kierkegaard: A Guide for the Perplexed, Clare Carlisle
Leibniz: A Guide for the Perplexed, Franklin Perkins
Levinas: A Guide for the Perplexed, B. C. Hutchens
Locke: A Guide for the Perplexed, Patricia Sheridan
Marx: A Guide for the Perplexed, John Sheed
Merleau-Ponty: A Guide for the Perplexed, Eric Matthews
Nietzsche: A Guide for the Perplexed, R. Kevin Hill
Plato: A Guide for the Perplexed, Gerald A. Press
Pragmatism: A Guide for the Perplexed, Robert B. Talisse and Scott F. Aikin
Quine: A Guide for the Perplexed, Gary Kemp
Relativism: A Guide for the Perplexed, Timothy Mosteller
Ricoeur: A Guide for the Perplexed, David Pellauer
Rousseau: A Guide for the Perplexed, Matthew Simpson
Sartre: A Guide for the Perplexed, Gary Cox
Schopenhauer: A Guide for the Perplexed, R. Raj Singh
Socrates: A Guide for the Perplexed, Sara Ahbel-Rappe
Spinoza: A Guide for the Perplexed, Charles Jarrett
The Stoics: A Guide for the Perplexed, M. Andrew Holowchak
Utilitarianism: A Guide for the Perplexed, Krister Bykvist

AQUINAS
A GUIDE FOR THE PERPLEXED

PETER S. EARDLEY AND CARL N. STILL

continuum

Continuum International Publishing Group

The Tower Building   80 Maiden Lane
11 York Road   Suite 704
London SE1 7NX   New York, NY 10038

www.continuumbooks.com

British Library Cataloguing-in-Publication Data
A catalogue record for this book is available from the British Library.

ISBN: HB: 978-0-8264-9879-3
       PB: 978-0-8264-9880-9

Library of Congress Cataloging-in-Publication Data
Eardley, Peter S.
Aquinas : a guide for the perplexed / Peter S. Eardley and Carl N. Still.
       p. cm.
Includes bibliographical references and index.
ISBN: 978-0-8264-9879-3
ISBN: 978-0-8264-9880-9
1. Thomas, Aquinas, Saint, 1225?–1274. I. Still, Carl N. II. Title.

B765.T54E19 2010
189'.4–dc22

2010012596

Typeset by Newgen Imaging Systems Pvt Ltd, Chennai, India
Printed and bound in India by Replika Press Pvt Ltd

For Stephen R. Eardley (1936–2009) and Dorothy V. Still (1935–2008), both of whom passed away while this book was being written.

Requiescant in pace.

CONTENTS

CHAPTER 1

INTRODUCTION

Thomas Aquinas is so central a figure in the history of philosophy that one may be surprised that he is not better known than he is. There are a number of reasons for this obscurity. He is almost certainly the best known and arguably the most influential of all the medieval Christian theologians of the scholastic period (1100–1350). Yet medieval philosophy has been among the most neglected of all major periods of Western philosophy. The very term 'medieval' is pejorative and implies that this vast 'middle age' was a hiatus between the luminous periods of Greco-Roman antiquity and the Italian Renaissance. Despite the achievements of the medieval period, which include the founding of universities and the construction of Gothic cathedrals, the term 'medieval' still suggests a chaotic and unenlightened time. Until the twentieth century, it was widely believed that medieval philosophy offered little in the way of original thought, since it was shaped by religious commitments. Generations of scholars have profoundly altered that impression, but there can be no denying that the great medieval philosophers were actually theologians and sought to harmonize the truths of philosophy with the doctrines of faith. Aquinas is no exception to this. In studying Aquinas, then, we are dealing with a medieval Catholic theologian. While much in his thought will be familiar, thanks in part to the persistence of Catholicism in the world today, other aspects will seem peculiar to the point of being all but unintelligible. Our goal will be to make these peculiar aspects more intelligible. This will not of course render them credible in every case or to every reader. But we hope to show why Aquinas's conclusions seemed credible to him, and why they still command attention and respect in many quarters today.

Why is Aquinas difficult to understand? It is certainly not because his writing is obscure. In contrast to many famous philosophers, Aquinas is a remarkably clear and concise writer. Unlike St. Augustine (354–430), Aquinas is not an accomplished literary stylist; unlike Duns Scotus (1265/66–1308), he does not pursue metaphysical subtleties to the vanishing point. Nor does his vocabulary pose any special problems. Apart from some technical terms that we will introduce along the way, Aquinas deals in the language common to the scholastic thought of his day. Nor does Aquinas introduce any new genres or topics otherwise unknown among medieval theologians. The problem is not one of style but of substance: Aquinas strikes many readers as hard to understand because of the sheer depth of his thinking. Aquinas probes deeply into whatever issue he confronts, and in so doing he produces new insights. Some of his insights have been celebrated for some time among scholars, while others have gained attention only recently. Etienne Gilson, for instance, was impressed by Aquinas's theory that the term 'being' names not only the essence of something, but its act of existing. More recently, Anthony Kenny has insisted that Aquinas's analysis of the mind is far more important, though far less studied, than his treatment of being.[1] Aquinas's insights have not been exhausted, and specialists continue to debate not only the relative merits of his positions, but in some cases even how to interpret his position on certain issues.

In the present volume we will illustrate Aquinas's depth with respect to five topics prominent in his thought: being, soul, knowledge, happiness and the common good. When Aquinas addresses each of these, he builds on previous philosophical thought and seeks to integrate it with Christian faith. For instance, with regard to being (*ens*), Aquinas accepts classical arguments that that there is an original being on which all other beings depend; but he then attempts to unite this philosophical concept of a first being with the Judeo-Christian concept of God. When he turns to soul (*anima*), he aims to show that the soul is united to the body in such a way that they form together a single person; yet the soul is so distinct from the body that it can exist apart from it. Without a philosophical basis for the soul's immortality, Aquinas thinks, the Christian promise of salvation would ring hollow. Regarding his theory of cognition, Aquinas premises that all knowledge (*scientia*) begins with perception by the senses, yet such knowledge must be adapted from these humble origins to consider immaterial beings, including God. Thus Aquinas's famous theory of analogy is born. From Aristotle (384–322 BC) he borrows the notion that happiness (*felicitas*) is the supreme goal of human life, but contends that no happiness enjoyed in this life can answer to the beatitude (*beatitudo*) of endless life with God. When it comes to the common good made possible by the state, Aquinas seeks to find in the best worldly polity a model compatible with the kingdom of heaven, in which perfect happiness is to be realized.

THE LIFE OF AQUINAS

Aquinas was born in 1224 or 1225 at Roccasecca in the region of Naples, Italy. His life of intense religious and scholarly activity was spent in various parts of his native Italy with three periods in Paris and another in Germany. As the youngest son of a knight with connections to Emperor Frederick II, Thomas became an oblate of the great Benedictine abbey of Monte Cassino. Although his family expected him to become a monk there, Thomas surprised them by his interest in the new Order of Preachers, commonly known as the Dominicans. When Thomas joined the Dominicans in 1244, his family confined him at home, hoping to break his will. When these attempts proved futile, the young Aquinas was allowed to return to the Dominicans, who promptly sent him to the centre of theological learning of the day – the University of Paris.

At Paris Thomas had the good fortune of studying under the leading light among Dominican theologians, Albert the Great (*ca.* 1200–1280). Thomas so impressed Albert that after 4 years in Paris (1245–1248), Albert took him along to the Dominican house of study (*studium*) at Cologne (1248–1252) as a student and assistant. The association with Albert was auspicious for Thomas, as Albert was in many ways a model of what Thomas aspired to be. While supervising his commentary on biblical books, Albert introduced Thomas to the works of Aristotle, among others. Known as 'the Philosopher' (*philosophus*) among the medieval scholastics, Aristotle would have an immense influence on Aquinas, who went on to write commentaries on 12 works by Aristotle. With the conclusion of his studies in Cologne, Thomas returned to Paris to complete his theological education (1252–1256). During this time he wrote the medieval equivalent of the modern doctoral dissertation: a commentary on the four-volume textbook known as the *Sentences* (*Sententiae*) by the twelfth century theologian Peter Lombard (*ca.* 1100–1160).[2]

With the conclusion of these studies Aquinas received the designation of 'master of theology' and was appointed to a teaching position in Paris in 1256. This would be the first of two appointments as 'regent master' – similar to holding a professorial chair today – at Paris. In 1259, Aquinas returned to Italy, where he would spend nearly ten years teaching at Naples, Orvieto and Rome. During these years Aquinas's scholarly work was in full swing: he was lecturing on the Bible, writing commentaries on Aristotle, and engaging in university 'disputations' on philosophical and theological topics. He also began the two largest-scale works of his career: the *Summa contra gentiles* (Summa against the Unbelievers) and the *Summa theologiae* (Summa of Theology). The summa was a medieval genre that attempted to expound all Christian doctrine in an organized way. Aquinas is exceptional in writing two summas, but the two works have rather different purposes. In the *Summa contra gentiles*, Aquinas relies on philosophical reasoning alone to meet objections to Christian faith, while in the *Summa theologiae* he attempts his most ambitious integration of reason and faith. Although unfinished at the time of his death, the *Summa theologiae* stands as a monument to the medieval mind, much like Dante's *Divine Comedy*, in which there is 'a place for everything and everything in the right place'.[3] Although Aquinas never had the chance to teach the *Summa theologiae* to his students, he tells us it was intended for theological beginners; today the work is frequently studied in philosophy courses, since it includes the writings for which Aquinas is best known: the 'five ways' of proving the existence of God, his discussion of the human being as a unity of soul and body, his treatment of happiness as a supernatural destiny for all human beings, and his exposition of natural law. We will examine each of these themes in separate chapters.

In 1268 Aquinas was called back to Paris for a second regency in theology. Tensions were running high at the university between philosophers who followed Aristotle, even when he contradicted Christian teaching, and theologians who rejected Aristotle as incompatible with Christianity. Two of the most controversial issues at the time concerned the origin of the world and the status of the human intellect. Aristotle had concluded that the world is eternal, while Christian theology was built on the biblical principle that God created the world in time. Further, while Christian doctrine required that each human being have his own rational soul as the basis for salvation, some philosophers at the University of Paris followed the

Muslim philosopher Ibn Rushd, known to the Latin west as Averroes (*ca.* 1126–1198). The latter's interpretation of Aristotle concluded that the intellect must be separate from matter. If the human intellect is totally immaterial, Averroes thought, there will be only one such intellect; but a single, immaterial intellect makes immortality impossible for individual souls. During his second Parisian regency (1268–1272), Aquinas wrote two separate treatises addressing these two contentious issues. He also continued work on the second and largest part of his *Summa theologiae*, which deals with happiness, natural law, and moral virtues – all of which are discussed in Chapter 5.

In 1272 Aquinas returned to Naples to serve as a regent master there. Residing near the home of his youth, Aquinas continued his work on the third part of the *Summa theologiae*. After composing the first 90 Questions, however, he abruptly stopped writing in December 1273. He reported that he had experienced a mystical vision, revealing that his work was as insignificant as straw compared to what he had seen. Aquinas did not live much longer after he ceased writing. On his way to a church council in Lyon in 1274, he was injured in an accident from which he never recovered. He died at a monastery in Fossanuova, south of Rome, on 7 March 1274. While some of his teachings were under suspicion during and shortly after his lifetime, Aquinas's reputation for theological wisdom and for personal sanctity grew over time. He was canonized by Pope John XXII in 1323. He would eventually be recognized as a 'Doctor' (teacher) of the Catholic church in 1567, though he is often referred to as the 'Common Doctor' (*Doctor communis*), an honorific title indicating that his teaching belongs not only to his Order but to the whole church.

FAITH AND REASON

Perhaps no theme is more persistent in medieval thought than the challenge of reconciling human reason with religious faith. Aquinas stands out among medieval thinkers for his synthesis of faith and reason. Before looking closely at major themes in Aquinas's thought, we will begin with an overview of his perspective on faith and reason.

Now faith and reason are separate modes of knowing, although they can overlap. Aquinas illustrates the overlap with the example of the existence of God. God's existence is an article of faith for the believer, while for the philosopher it is a conclusion of argumentation. The same truth can thus be known by believing or by reasoning. In some matters, however, faith and reason appear to reach opposed conclusions: as we noted earlier, Aristotle posited the eternity of the world, citing for example the principle that every motion presupposes a prior motion.[4] But the account of creation in Genesis holds that the world was created by God in time, specifically six days. Can there be contradictory truths in different fields of knowledge? Aquinas rejects this as impossible.

This brings us to a second principle: truths of reason cannot contradict truths of faith. It may seem that truths of reason are more secure than those of faith because they are reached by careful reasoning that can be verified time and again by different people. As much as he respects the power of reason, however, Aquinas cannot accept its superiority to faith, since to do so would be to elevate the human mind above the divine mind, which is the source of the truths of faith. The human mind is both limited in its grasp and fallible in its operation; the divine mind, by contrast, is unlimited and infallible. It would therefore be a mistake to prefer the conclusions of human reason to the revealed truths of faith.

Does this mean that faith leaves little or no scope for reason to discover anything new? As we shall see in more detail below, nothing could be further from the truth. While faith is characterized by certainty because it is based on a revelation from God, the believer grasps the truth but does not necessarily have knowledge of it. That is, faith has the certainty that characterizes knowledge, but does not 'see' its object as knowledge does. Consequently, the believer may *grasp* more – the Christian knows that God comprises a Trinity of persons, for example, not just a singular divinity – but *understand* less than the philosopher. Aquinas himself was neither a simple believer nor a pure philosopher, but a philosophical theologian. All of his work presupposes the truths of faith, yet Aquinas explores these truths with the help of philosophical skills developed by pre-Christian and non-Christian thinkers. Although reasoning would not have been able to discover the fundamental truths of faith, virtually all aspects of faith can be understood better by means of disciplined reasoning. Aquinas's work stands as a monument of such reasoning.

In the present study we do not deal directly with the purely theological themes in Aquinas's work such as the incarnation and saving work of Christ, the sacraments of the Catholic church, or other aspects of Aquinas's dogmatic theology. Aquinas's theology does not appear directly in most of the philosophical discussions we examine, but it is present implicitly. If we hope to understand Aquinas's thinking about any given topic, we need to keep in mind the larger theological framework in which he is working. We must also be careful to avoid the assumption that Aquinas ever writes purely as a philosopher. Consider his relationship to Aristotle, who more than any other philosopher exemplifies for Aquinas philosophical knowledge based on observation and reasoning. He agrees with Aristotle that the human being must be regarded as a unity of soul and body; that human knowledge begins with our sensory perceptions of the world around us; that we must acquire virtues through repeated effort; and on numerous other points. As learned and respectful a commentator on Aristotle as he is, though, Aquinas never hesitates to disagree with his philosophical predecessor when the latter's conclusions run counter to Christian faith. For while Aristotle has a concept of God as prime mover, he has no notion of the personal God in whom the Christian has faith. Aristotle distinguishes soul from body in human beings, but he stops short of demonstrating that the human soul is separable from its body and will survive its death. Aristotle correctly identifies happiness as the goal of human life, but his account of happiness in our present condition does not answer to the happiness for which we were created. On all these points Aquinas is guided by Aristotle's lead, but must transcend the limits of his conclusions. The theological worldview that shapes Aquinas's thought requires nothing less.

In this sense it seems dubious to think of Aquinas simply as an 'Aristotelian', though he is often described that way. The label is apt inasmuch as Aristotle was the pre-eminent philosophical authority in Aquinas's time, and Aquinas clearly follows Aristotle on any number of watershed issues in philosophy. The description seems less fitting, though, when we notice how many other authorities Aquinas relies on in his work. While he cites Plato mostly to criticize him, Aquinas is indebted to a number of neo-Platonists, who hardly belong in the same philosophical camp as Aristotle. His work as a Christian theologian stretches his Aristotelian identity even further, as he relies on the Bible and a host of Christian writers as authorities.[5] Rather like Virgil to Dante in *Purgatory*, the pagan sage can lead the Christian pilgrim only so far, but then must depart. Aristotle is 'the Philosopher' to Aquinas, as to other medieval scholastics, but by the time Aquinas is finished interpreting him, the Philosopher's thought has been transformed into a new synthesis.

READING AQUINAS

The purpose of any such guide as this one is to serve as an introduction, and an accompaniment, to reading Thomas Aquinas's own writings. As we have noted, Aquinas wrote various kinds of works, but we will focus – primarily but not exclusively – on the *Summa theologiae*, for three reasons. First, the *Summa theologiae* is the best known of all of Aquinas's works. It is likely, then, that readers who have already encountered Aquinas have done so in the form of the *Summa theologiae*. Second, although it is unfinished, the *Summa theologiae* is Aquinas's *magnum opus*. While it is not his only *Summa*, it is a later and more mature work than either the *Summa contra gentiles* or his commentary on the *Sentences*. Aquinas did not alter his positions much on major issues over the course of his career, but he did refine the presentation of his views. The *Summa theologiae* typically captures Aquinas' final position on a given question. Third, precisely because it is a *summa*, the discussions are presented in summary form. While this approach lacks the richness of the accounts to be found in some of his other works, it is also far easier for the novice to understand. As occasion warrants, we will point to passages in other works that illumine discussions in the *Summa theologiae*.

The *Summa theologiae* is a work of vast scope and intricate structure. As noted earlier, it is divided into three parts; each part is made up of 'questions'; and each question is composed of 'articles', which pose a question within the larger question. Among the three parts, there are 512 questions.[6] For example, the very first question in the First Part of the *Summa theologiae* concerns the nature and extent of sacred doctrine, and the first article in that question asks, 'Is sacred doctrine necessary?' The articles in the *Summa theologiae* also have a distinct structure reflecting the disputation style of teaching at medieval universities. In response to any question, arguments can be marshaled for either the affirmative or the negative. Students were charged with providing arguments on one side or another of any issue, to which the master would respond in a 'determination' (*determinatio*) offering the resolution. In the *Summa theologiae*, the arguments on both sides are limited to the opposite of Aquinas's own position, which begins with the words 'I answer that' (*respondeo*). After Aquinas has provided his response to the question, he replies to each of the opening arguments, indicating what truth it contained and how it went wrong in its assessment of the issue.

After the opening arguments (misleadingly called 'objections' in some translations) Aquinas cites authorities contradicting these arguments (*sed contra*), often from the Bible or a Christian author, but sometimes from a pagan authority like Aristotle. Then he draws a conclusion. While the *sed contra* is an important part of each article in the *Summa theologiae*, it is not intended to be an argument, and should not be taken as one. The medievals respected authorities, so a statement by an acknowledged authority contradicting a reasoned argument carried some weight. It signalled that the argument just offered was not the final word on the subject. However, Aquinas knows well that the argument from authority is the weakest of arguments. For this reason, the discussion does not terminate with the citation of an authority. Instead, the *sed contra* sets the stage for the master to enter with his own voice to resolve the issue, giving due consideration to both sides. The 'scholastic method' was an enormously demanding exercise for the master or, in the case of the *Summa theologiae*, for the author. To get a sense of what it might have been like to be the master in such an exercise, pause after reading Aquinas's response in any article in the *Summa*, then reread the opening arguments, and try to surmise how he will reply to each argument. When you can reliably guess Aquinas's reply, you will know that you are beginning to figure out how Aquinas thinks.

There are various conventions for citing Aquinas's *Summa theologiae*. In the notes to each chapter, we will cite the work using the internal divisions mentioned above: part, question and article. Thus, *ST* I, q. 2, a. 1 refers to part one, question 2, article 1. The further specification 'arg. 1' refers to the first of the opening arguments (numbered in the text); 'sc' refers to the 'sed contra'; 'corp.' refers to the body (*corpus*) of the article, or the master's response; and 'ad 1' refers to the reply to the first argument. While there are several English translations of the *Summa theologiae*, we provide our own translations based on the Leonine critical edition, though using the authoritative English Dominican translation as a model and updating it as necessary. In the Bibliography at the end of this book, we have provided a recommended list of English translations, as well as Latin editions of Aquinas's works for those who can benefit by consulting them. In addition to these primary materials, we also provide a select bibliography of modern scholarly works that we have found helpful in illuminating Aquinas on various points. While there is a vast secondary literature on Aquinas, and many important studies in languages other than English, we have focused on publications in English for purposes of this volume. We hope that these references will be useful to students writing on Aquinas, and to interested readers wishing to pursue further the interpretations and controversies discussed here.

CHAPTER 2

METAPHYSICS

Aquinas regards metaphysics as the study of being *qua* being, which is to say, the study of being as such (*ens inquantum ens*). Everything that exists can obviously be studied and, accordingly, made the subject of a science. Beings insofar as they are living are the subject of biology, while beings insofar as they are in motion are the subject matter of physics, to name two examples of disciplines that most moderns would recognize as legitimate sciences. Contemporary readers might be surprised to discover, however, that in addition to disciplines such as biology, physics, psychology and astronomy, Aquinas also regarded what many today would regard as purely *philosophical* subjects – such as metaphysics and ethics – as sciences (*scientiae*). This claim is likely to seem odd to the modern reader, who tends to associate the term 'science' in a very strict sense with the natural sciences. However, in holding the view that metaphysics is a science, Aquinas was just thinking like a good Aristotelian, for whom any mode of inquiry that involves reasoning from principles to conclusions is a *scientia*. Hence, even ethics is a science on the Aristotelian model to which Aquinas subscribes. Of all the sciences, however, metaphysics is unique. Why? Because its subject matter cuts across all of the other disciplines, as it were, in order to study being in abstraction from embodiment, motion and so on, so as to capture its most fundamental properties. It also deals with the nature and existence of the highest being in existence – God – who is both the first cause and very ground of being.

GOD AND METAPHYSICS

The root of the Latin term *scientia* is the verb *scire*, which means 'to know' or 'to understand', but in its earliest sense meant 'to get to the bottom of the matter' or to uncover its roots.[1] Hence, science for the medievals had to do in the first instance with discovering the causes of things. This is in a sense true of how moderns continue to understand the practice of science. To have scientific knowledge of some feature of the world, most of us would agree, involves an ability to provide an account of what brings it into being, that is, to come to know its cause in some sense. Where we differ from the medievals most markedly is in our insistence that the appropriate and indeed only method for achieving such knowledge is by means of observation and measurement. We tend to think, in other words, that the only type of knowledge that counts as scientific is what we might call 'empiriological'.[2]

Now, the medievals agreed that the empiriological mode of investigation was a valid and important one. But, following Aristotle, they were emphatic in their belief that there was more to understanding some feature of the world than merely to uncover what brought it into existence, which was only one mode of explaining it. Moreover, they rejected the notion that the subject matter of science should be limited to what is observable, and therefore material. As one commentator has put it, science for a medieval thinker such as Aquinas did 'not aim simply at empiriological knowledge gained through controlled observation and measurement of the physical world, but knowledge of the very being and structure of things'.[3]

Following Aristotle, Aquinas thought that there are four ways to provide an adequate, scientific explanation (*causa*) for every feature of the world.[4] First, one can explain something – let us call it x – by pointing to the physical stuff out of which it is made. This is called its material cause. Second, it is possible to explain x by giving a rational account of its internal structure or organizing principle. This is called its formal cause because it articulates the form or 'whatness' (*quidditas*) of x. Third, one can provide a scientific explanation for something by pointing to who or what brought it into existence or, to put it in scholastic terms, of 'the first principle of change or rest'. This explanation is commonly called the efficient cause of x, because it articulates the principle that effected x's coming into existence. Finally, it is possible to give a scientific explanation for x, so Thomas thinks, by pointing to its purpose or function. This is traditionally known as its final cause, because it articulates x's purpose or aim (*finis*).

To fill out the foregoing, let us take a less abstract example to illustrate the four types of causes, one that, in fact, both Aristotle and Aquinas use: that of a silver goblet. If one were an inquisitive child that had never encountered such an object before, there are four questions one might ask about it. One would probably enquire, first and foremost, into its quiddity (*quidditas*).[5] One would probably ask: 'what is it?' And the answer would be something along the lines of: 'a physical object of a semi-rounded shape suitable for putting to the lips'. This would be its formal explanation. Now, we have to be careful to avoid strictly equating the form of something with its *physical* form or shape. The form or quiddity that the goblet possesses – its 'goblet-ness', if you will – is the essence that is common to all goblets, regardless of their size, colour, texture and so on. It is both the goblet's organizing principle and, once apprehended by knowing subjects such as ourselves, an abstract universal concept. Admittedly, in the case of the goblet, it is tempting to say that its physical shape is so closely bound up with its quiddity that its form, in an important sense, just *is* that it is a certain object of a certain physical shape. We should, however, resist this temptation. Regardless of how bound up with its physicality the definition of such an object is, the essence or definition *itself* is non-physical; otherwise we would be able to fully capture it in the way that we capture other physical objects: by drawing it, for example. Obviously this is not possible. We may be able to draw an *instance* of 'goblet-ness', but we can never adequately capture, in a material way, goblet-ness as such.

The second obvious question that an inquisitive child might ask is: 'what is it for?' And the answer to this question will obviously have to do with the purpose for which it was designed, namely, 'to hold liquid for the purpose of transferring to the human mouth'. This, of course, would be its final cause. A child might then ask what it was made of, to which one would provide the goblet's material cause, in this case, 'silver'. Finally, one might ask after the goblet's efficient cause, the answer to which would be something like: 'John the craftsman.'

Now, it is easy enough for most contemporary readers to concede that man-made objects are produced for a purpose. Nautical engineers *usually* build yachts for the purpose of traversing a body of water and medical scientists *usually* produce drugs for the purpose of curing or alleviating physical or mental illnesses. Where many moderns might be tempted to part company with Aristotle and Aquinas is in the assumption that there are objective purposes to *organic* beings – imposed by nature in the case of Aristotle, and by God in the case of Aquinas. For in the post-Darwinian age, is it not the case that everything in nature has come into being by chance and therefore has no objective purpose whatsoever? Aquinas and Aristotle would have emphatically disagreed with this Darwinian notion. Rather, on their view, the universe exhibits law-like regularity and, accordingly, is a purposeful and intelligible place.

We now have a better idea of why metaphysics is a science for Aquinas, and why it has to do with God. It is a mode of inquiry – a *scientia* – that seeks to understand being as such. But to adequately explain any phenomenon in a scientific sense, one must explain it through its causes. Since God is, for Thomas, the ultimate cause of all reality and indeed the very ground of being, as we shall see in a moment, he is therefore relevant to metaphysics which, to the extent that it investigates being and its causes and principles, can be considered a science. Indeed, so Thomas thinks, not only is metaphysics a science, but its study also leads to the highest sort of wisdom. As Aquinas puts it in his commentary on Aristotle's *Metaphysics*, 'It follows that the science treating of first causes seems to be the supreme ruler of all the others.'[6] Given this view, it is hardly surprising that Aquinas also regards metaphysics as a type of 'divine science' (*divina scientia*).[7]

Now, to the extent that God is being itself, and metaphysics is the study of being *qua* being, we might say that God is the principle of the subject of metaphysics.[8] How can we come to know such an inscrutable being? The short answer is: insofar as he reveals himself, which he does in two ways: (1) through scripture (*sacra pagina*), and (2) by means of his effects in the world. It is through the latter means that the metaphysician comes to understand God. Indeed, Aquinas is fond of quoting Paul's Epistle to the Romans where the Apostle famously writes: 'the invisible things of God are clearly seen, being understood by the things that are made'. The belief that the study of the natural world reveals inferential knowledge about God played a seminal role in the emergence of modern science.[10] But it was initially the province of the 'philosophers' (*philosophi*), who study God as he is Creator and source of all things, as opposed to the 'theologians' (*theologi*), who study God as he is in himself, and as he reveals himself through scripture.[11]

In order to show that God is self-subsistent being and therefore the principle of the subject of metaphysics, we need to demonstrate that he actually exists. Once we do this, we will be able to infer certain things about him, among them that he is the ground of all being. But it is necessary to provide philosophical demonstrations for God's existence if we are going to make valid inferences about his nature. Aquinas was undoubtedly possessed of a deep religious faith. But as a scholar and a theologian he refused simply to take God's existence on faith. Rather, he thought that this could be demonstrated to the satisfaction of rational people.

There are different attitudes to the question of God's existence today, and this was equally true of Thomas's time. There have always been those, for example, who see very little reason to suppose the existence of a transcendent being, much less one with the personal attributes ascribed to the God of the Judeo-Christian and Islamic traditions. Often, this attitude is informed by the problem of evil, which generates for some people a major obstacle to belief in God. On this view, the existence of evil demonstrates either that God does not exist, or else he is lacking omnipotence, omnibenevolence or both. Surely, so the argument goes, the fact that people murder and rape each other (examples of moral evil) and that earthquakes and cancer kill people (examples of natural evils) is fairly conclusive proof of one of several possible alternatives. Either God does not exist; or he does exist but is impotent to do anything to prevent such evils; or he *does* have the power to prevent such evils, but does not wish to. If God exists at all, he is either good but impotent, or omnipotent but sadistic.[12]

The need to posit the existence of God is also seen by some as obsolete on modern scientific grounds. Prior to Darwin, the apparent elegance of the universe suggested that it was the product of a grand designer. Darwin showed, however, that what *appears* to be the product of design in the natural world was more likely the product of random natural selection, that is, of chance.[13] Further to this, while there may be 'gaps' in our knowledge of the world, so this argument goes, we still do not have reason to posit God's existence to explain any of them. Our knowledge is constantly progressing, and we have no reason to think that science will not provide us with all of the answers in the future. There is no need to posit, so this argument concludes, a 'God of the gaps'.[14] Unsurprisingly, arguments such as these typically generate various forms of atheism and agnosticism.

Now, there is another group that is sympathetic to the skepticism of the atheists vis à vis the notion that God's existence can be proven. Unlike atheists, however, this group *does* believe that God exists – they just do not think that God's existence can be rationally demonstrated. Rather, it must be taken on faith. For some, this sort of fideism is associated with the belief that the human ability to achieve any kind of truth has been so corrupted by original sin that we cannot possibly hope to have indisputable, demonstrative knowledge about such things as the existence of God.[15] For others, faith must take priority over reason because God's essence is identical with his existence. But because we cannot know by natural reason what God's essence consists of, neither can we rationally demonstrate his existence.[16] Such views have been associated with such fourteenth-century theologians as William of Ockham (*ca.* 1285–1347), and such Protestant Reformers as Martin Luther (1483–1546) and John Calvin (1509–1564). Even granting that what we call fideism has changed throughout history, it is nonetheless true that Aquinas was familiar with the basic claim that faith must take precedence over reason when it assenting to the existence of God.[17]

Aquinas will have no truck with any of these views. The problem of evil in no way proves that God does not exist, so Thomas thinks, or that his goodness and omnipotence are incompatible. This is because evil is nothing more than a privation. Just as darkness is merely an absence of light, so evil is merely an absence of goodness.[18] To this extent, God's omnipotence can be demonstrated from the fact that he creates everything that exists, and to the extent that everything that exists is good, we are entitled to consider him omnibenevolent.[19] Likewise, as we shall see in a moment, if God exists, then there are ways to infer that he is rational creator. And if he is rational, then the world must be a purposeful place in which final causes can be discerned.[20] Furthermore, if everything is good, then it has being. And if it has being, then it participates, to a greater or lesser degree, in the pure actuality that is the divine essence. This demonstrates that God is not only the efficient cause of all things – and the governor of the universe – but their final cause as well.

Aquinas is equally critical of the fideistic claim that, because God's essence is his existence, and because we cannot know the former in this life, neither can we demonstrate the latter. And this is not because he rejects the claim that God's essence and his existence are one and the same – quite the contrary. Nor is it to suggest that, on Thomas's view, we can know the very essence of God in this life, for we cannot. This is, in part, because our intellects are finite and God is infinite, which generates obvious epistemological problems.[21]

Rather, where Aquinas fundamentally disagrees with the fideistic position is in his belief that such a limitation acts as an impediment to giving a rational demonstration of God's existence. For while we may not be able to fully appreciate *what* God is in this life, so Thomas thinks, we can certainly come to know *that* he is, and we can do so by means of examining his effects. In the Thomistic idiom, we can provide a *quia* demonstration of God's existence, or a proof that proceeds from effects to causes, if not a *propter quid* demonstration, or a proof that proceeds from cause to effect. The latter type of demonstration is impossible with respect to God, because it would involve our having real knowledge of the divine essence in this life-time, which is impossible.[22] Obviously it would be better to know *what* God is, and therefore be able to employ a *propter quid* demonstration, rather than to know merely *that* he is. In this life, however, we must be content with the latter. And in any case, *quia* demonstrations are better than nothing if one is seeking to establish rational grounds on which to believe in God.

From the foregoing it will come as little surprise to discover that Aquinas rejects St. Anselm's famous Ontological Argument. In the eleventh century, the Benedictine monk had attempted to devise a very simple proof for the existence of God, which he began by urging readers to look within themselves, as it were, in order to contemplate the divine nature.[23] His motive was to arrive at a rational understanding of those matters that he took on faith – faith seeking understanding (*fides quaerens intellectum*). 'Look favorably upon us, O Lord; hear us, enlighten us, show yourself to us.'[24] Anselm's appeal to look into 'the chamber of the mind', as opposed to the external world, for evidence of the existence of God places his argument into the category of *proper quid* or *a priori* demonstrations inasmuch as it is rooted purely in a *definition* of God.[25]

When religious believers retreat into themselves, according to Anselm, they notice that faith has given them a certain conception of God as 'something than which nothing greater can be thought' (*aliquid quo nihil maius cogitari possit*).[26] This is a reasonable definition that everyone, even the atheist, can acknowledge. What the atheist denies, of course, is that the being to which this definition points exists outside the mind as well. God is like a unicorn or the Tooth Fairy – beings of which I can *conceive*, but which exist solely as a product of my imagination. Anselm's response is that the concept 'God' is of an entirely different order than the concepts of 'unicorn' and 'Tooth Fairy'. This is because there is no requirement in the definition of either of these fictional beings that they be perfect or complete. Put otherwise, there is absolutely no contradiction in asserting that unicorns and Tooth Fairies are mere products of the imagination, because perfection or absolute completion does not factor into their fundamental natures as they are commonly conceived. One *does* contradict oneself, however, if one asserts of the most perfect being conceivable – God – that he is lacking existence. For clearly, if he is lacking existence, then he is most certainly *not* the most perfect being conceivable.

The ontological argument, then, is rooted in the assumption that once someone concedes that they have in their *minds* the concept of God as 'something than which nothing greater can be thought' – which the atheist *must* grant, since he cannot deny the existence of what he does not understand – they will have to concede, on pain of contradiction, that God exists not just in the mind, but outside the mind as well. This is because if God did *not* possess extra-mental existence, or real being outside the mind, he would not *be* 'something than which nothing greater can be thought'. How then is it even possible for the atheist to deny God's existence? Anselm thinks that when the atheist thinks or speaks the words 'God does not exist', what he is actually doing is paying insufficient attention to the meaning of what he is saying.[27] Anselm's argument is effectively as follows:

(P1) God is 'that than which nothing greater can be thought'.
(P2) Such a being can exist in the mind alone, or in the mind and in reality.
(P3) However, it is greater to exist in the mind and in reality than in the mind alone.
(P4) Therefore, God must exist in the mind *and* in reality; otherwise, he would not *be* 'that than which nothing greater can be thought'.

Aquinas was very familiar with Anselm's argument, but he did not accept it, mainly because he thought that it involved an illicit transition from the logical realm to the realm of actually existing beings. The most that can be demonstrated about God if he is signified as 'something than which nothing greater can be thought' is that such a concept exists in the mind.[28] It is not, of course, that Aquinas sides with the atheist against Anselm. Rather, it is that Aquinas finds such proofs as the ontological argument that appeal to some innate idea of God inadequate to do what they purport to do.

The data on which to base valid proofs for God's existence, so Thomas thinks, must be rooted in sense-experience. His famous 'Five Ways' (*quinque viae*) therefore all start from some feature of the external world, and argue that the only way that this feature can be adequately explained is to posit the existence of some being that acts as its ultimate cause. Because they look to the world for evidence of the existence of God, the Five Ways are sometimes considered variations of the 'cosmological argument' for God's existence. None of the actual arguments is original with Aquinas. Rather, they can all be found in his predecessors.

Of all the proofs, Aquinas is arguably fondest of the so-called First Way, also sometimes called the proof from change or motion. Aquinas likes this argument because it is based on a very obvious and undeniable feature of the external world: material things change. That is, they go from potentially being x to actually being x. In temperate regions of the globe, for example, the leaves on deciduous trees change from being green to becoming various hues of red, yellow and orange in the autumn. They go, that is, from being potentially red-orange-yellow in colour although actually green, to being actually red-orange-yellow and no longer green. Eventually, of course, they fall off the tree altogether and the process begins again in the spring. There are countless examples of this sort of change. That the world that is available to the senses is constantly in this state of flux or becoming is such a common feature of it that Aquinas calls this proof 'very clear' (*manifestior*).

How does the very obvious fact that some things move suggest that God exists? Because positing a prime mover is the only reasonable way to provide an ultimate explanation for the existence of motion. For Thomas, as for Aristotle, there can be no such thing as self-motion. This is because the process we call change or motion involves the reduction of something from potentiality to actuality, as we saw in the case of the leaves a moment ago. But for something to change itself, it would have to be both x and not-x at the same time and in the same respect, and this is clearly impossible. The shirt I am now wearing is either white or not white, but it cannot be both at the same time and in the same respect; if this were the case it would possess contradictory properties at one and the same time. It is perfectly true, of course, that although my shirt is actually white at this moment it is also *potentially* red or blue, but that is another matter. It follows therefore that nothing can change itself or reduce itself from potentiality to actuality. As Aquinas might put it, whatever is moved must be moved by something else (*omne quod movetur ab alio movetur*). However there cannot exist an infinity of movers, since if there *were* such an infinity, there would be no first mover, and if there were no first mover, there would accordingly be no motion in the world. Because there clearly *is* motion in the world, there must be some First Mover who is himself unmoved. This, according to Aquinas, is God.[29]

The Second Way, or the proof from efficient causality, closely resembles the First. Its starting point, however, is not derived from the fact of motion in the world. Rather, it is that 'we find in sensible things an order of efficient causality.'[30] Now, these two types of causation are close enough that Aristotle, who is the original source of the First Way, did not recognize any distinction between them. For him, a moving cause just *is* that which actualizes some potentiality and therefore, in a sense, just reduces to an efficient cause. Aquinas, however, was influenced on this, as he was in other ways, by the great Islamic philosopher Ibn Sīnā (980–1037) – or as the Latin west knew him, Avicenna – who *did* draw a distinction between moving causes and efficient causes, the latter of which impart existence or being to things. Aquinas adopts this distinction and uses it to demonstrate that, to the extent that nothing can be the efficient cause of itself – since in order to do so, it would have to be both prior and posterior to itself: prior as efficient cause, and posterior as recipient – then everything must have a cause of its existence that is other than itself. In short, nothing can cause itself to exist. But this ordering of efficient causes cannot go on indefinitely, so Thomas thinks, for the same reasons that make an infinite regress in the order of moving causes impossible. At some point, there is the need to posit a first efficient cause which is itself uncaused if there are to be any intermediate causes. Since there clearly *are* intermediate efficient causes, there must clearly exist a first Uncaused Cause. This is God.[31]

The Third Way is also inspired by Ibn Sīnā , and is sometimes called the proof from contingency and necessity. Ibn Sīnā, who wrote in Arabic, claimed to have demonstrated in his proof that God is 'The Necessary of Existence' (wājib al-wujūd), and Aquinas adopts this idea. The argument is based on a very familiar feature of the world, namely, that things come into being, and pass out of being. They are born, and one day they die. This is true of everything to which we have access by means of our senses. One might say that the objects that comprise the material world are contingent, which is to say that the reason for their existence lies outside themselves. Following Ibn Sīnā, Aquinas calls such creatures 'possible beings', since it is of their very nature that they are both capable of existing and not existing. But clearly, so Thomas thinks, if they are dependent for their being on something outside themselves, then there was a point at which they did not exist. It follows from this that, if the universe were entirely comprised of possible beings, then nothing would exist right now – unless, that is, there were a being that was intrinsically necessary, that is, the reason for its own existence and who is the explanation for contingent creatures.[32]

The Fourth Way is taken from the degrees of perfection – or grades of being – in the world. It is an argument that is, if not literally defended in the Metaphysics, at least 'gathered from the words of Aristotle,' as Thomas puts it in the Summa contra gentiles.[33] It is based on the claim that beings in the world exhibit various degrees of goodness, truth, nobility and the like. A fully grown, healthy horse is more perfect, or 'better,' on Aquinas's metaphysical scheme, than a young or underdeveloped one. Likewise, so Thomas thinks, some propositions are truer than others and some actions 'nobler.' It is nobler to give money to charity, for example, than to squander it at the roulette table. In all sorts of ways, then, the world seems to exhibit degrees of 'more' and 'less' value. But such an ontology implies, according to Aquinas, some standard or maximum against which various things are measured as either 'better,' or 'truer' and so on. However, if there exist things that are 'hot' or 'hotter,' so Thomas thinks, there must be something that is 'hottest'. Likewise, if there are beings that are 'noble' and 'nobler', 'true' and 'truer', 'good' and 'better', there must be some being that is 'noblest', 'truest' and 'best', which is to say, a being that is 'maximum' (maxime ens) in every genus, and which is therefore the cause of every being in that genus. Aquinas calls this being God.[34]

The Fifth Way might be called the proof from the governance of the universe, and it is derived from the Eastern Christian theologian John Damascene (*ca.* 676–745). It is based on the observation that natural beings tend to act in a regular, law-like, deliberate way. They appear, that is, to exhibit intentional behaviour. Now, to act intentionally or deliberately is to act with an end or goal in view; it is to do something 'on purpose', as it were. Other events, of course, happen by chance, which is to say that they happen rarely and fail to exhibit intentionality. A clear example of intentional behaviour is deliberate human action, which is by definition goal-directed. When I deliberate about achieving x by means of y and set about choosing y, I am directing myself with a goal in view – the obtaining of x – that I regard as somehow 'good'. That I may be mistaken in my assessment of x is beside the point. It is sufficient, so Thomas thinks, that I regard it in some sense as worthy of pursuing (and therefore 'good') that my pursuit of it be considered purposeful or intentional.

Notice, however, that the pursuit of goodness, which is an abstract, universal object, implies rationality. My dog Jasper does not move towards her bowl of water because she thinks it would be 'good' to drink right now – or at any other time, for that matter. Indeed she cannot act under such a description because she cannot frame abstract thoughts such as 'x or y would be good to do.' Rather, she drinks water because, presumably, she is experiencing an immediate, visceral thirst that she desires to satisfy. Nonetheless, she in some sense moves herself because she possesses basic cognitive powers and is capable of making means/end calculations based on her cognitions. But how does one explain the purposeful behaviour of non-rational, organic beings like acorns and chicken eggs? How is it that they regularly strive for goals – that is, the 'good' – if they lack reason? The acorn *regularly* appears to strive to become an oak tree and the egg *regularly* inclines to hatching into a chicken. They do not do so by chance. Rather, that they do so regularly signals just the oppo-. site. Aquinas's answer is that if such creatures cannot direct themselves to such goals due to their lack of reason, then they must be directed by something else, 'for those things that do not have cognition (*cognitio*) do not tend to an end unless they are directed by something that has knowledge and intelligence, as the arrow is [directed to its end] by the archer'.[35] Such an intelligence, Aquinas thinks, is God.

ANALOGY OF BEING

Aquinas's five ways are all obviously rooted in the idea that certain features of the cosmos can only be explained if we posit a being who is subsistent, uncaused, self-necessary, perfect and rational. Moreover, all of these notions are related to the idea that, as the First Way quite clearly demonstrates, God is pure actuality or being. Since creatures are effects of God, they all, so Thomas thinks, reflect something of the divine nature. And if, as the proof from efficient causality seems to show, God is the first cause of being, then, to the extent that effects contain something of their causes, it follows that all creatures *qua* creatures must have some formal relation or likeness to God.

But a potential problem immediately arises: if God, as a transcendent cause, is self-subsistent being (*ipsum esse subsistens*) and pure actuality, in what sense can we even begin to talk about the *participation* of creatures in the divine being? What could limited, contingent, fallible creatures such as ourselves, for example, possibly have in common with God, and how do we even begin to articulate such a relationship? As Aquinas puts it in his early commentary on the *Sentences*: 'There is one being (*esse*) by which all things exist as by an efficient and exemplary principle; yet a different existence (*esse*) is present in each different thing by which this thing formally exists.'[36] Aquinas's doctrine of analogy (*analogia*) represents an attempt to solve the problem of how to talk about God meaningfully given that we cannot, in this life, penetrate the divine essence: 'to know self-subsistent being is natural to the divine intellect alone, and . . . is beyond the natural power of any created intellect, for no creature is its own being, since its being is participated.'[37]

Now, the metaphysical chasm between creatures and creator has led some to wonder how, and indeed whether, it is even *possible* to talk about the creator, much less capture his essence. Some in the Christian tradition have argued that God is so utterly transcendent that he is altogether inaccessible to human cognition. Such earlier Christian writers – mostly inspired by the mystical, neoplatonic tradition – as John Damascene (676–749) and John Scotus Eriugena (*ca.* 815–877) certainly thought this was the case. Indeed, they all would have emphatically agreed with the sixth-century mystical thinker Dionysius Areopagite when he claimed that 'God is beyond all being and knowledge.' While Aquinas recognizes the difficulties associated with cognizing the divine being, he nonetheless does think that it is possible for rational creatures to talk – and therefore to know something – about God in a meaningful, if limited, way. This is what the doctrine of analogy is designed to do. In order to understand the doctrine of analogy, it will perhaps be useful to consider a famous competing approach: the univocity of being.

Aquinas's famous successor, John Duns Scotus (1265/66–1308), claimed that there is only one kind of being in the world and that the terms we ascribe to God and creatures must therefore be univocal. Univocal predication, or the application of a 'name' (*nomen*) or term to two or more things in exactly the same sense, is necessary for Scotus because otherwise we could not have any knowledge of God. 'If you maintain that . . . the formal concept of what pertains to God is another notion, a disconcerting consequence ensues; namely that from the proper notion of anything found in creatures, nothing at all can be inferred about God, for the notion of what is in each is wholly different.'[38] For Scotus, then, unless we grant univocity to both God and creatures, we will not be able to comprehend anything about the divine essence, nor will we be able even to demonstrate the existence of God. This is because we cannot know that God exists without knowing what sort of being we are claiming existence for. Thus if we say that God has being and that individual humans possess being, it is necessary that we use the term 'being' in exactly the same sense. This holds true of other predicates common to God and creatures such as 'wisdom', 'goodness' and so on. If we do not mean the same thing by these terms when we predicate them of God and creatures, so Scotus thinks, then we cannot make any inferences from our knowledge of the latter to our knowledge of the former.[39]

Aquinas would have regarded the Scotistic view as an impossibility. This is because creatures are the effects of God, who is their efficient cause and who is accordingly responsible for endowing them with the specific form that they have. But unless the form that is endowed by the agent on the patient is *exactly* the same form, according to Aquinas, then we cannot speak about their effects in a univocal sense. Take the example of the sun and its effects. When I leave a cold drink in the sun it will, if not consumed quickly enough, become hot. Clearly this is because the sun is, to say the least, hot of its very form or nature, and the effect this tends to have on other things is to make them hot, as well. My now hot drink, by contrast, is not hot of its very form or nature, because prior to my leaving it in the sun, it was cold. In fact, my drink of its very form or nature is neither hot nor cold, except insofar as heat or cold modifies it. In other words, when I apply the term 'hot' to my drink, and also to the sun, I am using the term in a non-univocal sense.[40] Clearly the sense in both instances is *related*, but not identical.

The foregoing is equally true, so Thomas thinks, of God and his effects. God of his very form or essence is simple and unified while the forms he creates are multiple, complex and varied, for their attributes are distinct from their essences, as indeed their existence is distinct from their essence. As we will see in the following section, this is because all beings other than God have an existence that is distinct from their form or essence. We sometimes, for example, ascribe the predicate *wise* to human beings. But we certainly do not ascribe this predicate to *all* human beings. Wisdom, in the case of humans, is merely an attribute that some have, and others do not, and is entirely distinguishable from their essence. This is not the case with God. His wisdom, his being and his goodness are not separable, but intricate parts of his form, which contains all of these things because of his supereminent goodness. Hence, to apply predicates such as 'wise' and 'good' to both God and creatures univocally is impossible. This is not to suggest that certain terms cannot be used of both God and creatures, but only that they cannot be used in exactly the same sense given that the form of the creature is, at best, a pale reflection of the form in the creator.[41]

Now, God might be beyond our complete comprehension, but this does not mean that we must remain silent when talking about God, or resort exclusively to metaphors. Nor should we infer that if we cannot predicate univocal terms of both God and creatures that the only option that remains is to resort to equivocal predication: a type of semantic usage in which the same term is used in entirely different senses to refer to different objects. So, for example, when I say 'I am going to the bank', the term *bank* can in this context intelligibly mean either *the side of a river* or *the place where one keeps one's money*. Aquinas resists this mode of predication to capture the relation between human thought and speech and the transcendent reality of God for good reason. If the common terms that we apply to God and his creation are purely equivocal – if, for example, when we say 'God is wise' we mean something *entirely* different than when we say 'Solomon is wise' – then knowing anything about God will obviously be impossible. This is because, so Thomas thinks, whatever knowledge we can have about God we derive from creatures (*ex creaturis*). Accordingly, although we might be able to apply predicates such as 'wise' to God as *we* understand the term with reference to ourselves, they would nonetheless have no meaning in relation to him.[42]

For Aquinas, then, the only meaningful way to talk about God is by means of analogy (*analogia*) or proportion (*proportio*), a mode of predication mid-way between simple univocation and pure equivocation.[43] God is ultimately ineffable, but he nonetheless offers rational beings a glimpse into the divine nature through creating a diversity of perfections to which rational beings have access. Hence, human knowledge of perfections such as 'wisdom,' 'beauty' and 'being,' because they derive from a divine source, reflect and therefore provide knowledge of the Creator. Through the use of analogical predication, then, rational beings come to know something true, and not merely metaphorical, if not entirely adequate, about the divine nature.

Analogical predication can occur in two ways. It can either occur when a term is predicated of two different things in proportion to some third thing, or of two different things in relation to one another. Thus, to use Aquinas's example, in the first sense the term 'healthy' can be attributed to both medicine and urine, objects which, though different in form from another, are related in that both demonstrate commonality and difference. Commonality in that both are related to some third object – a 'healthy body' – but their mode of predication is distinct. When applied to urine, the term 'healthy' operates as a sign of a healthy body; when applied to medicine, on the other hand, it signifies the production of physical well-being. In other words, both uses of the term 'healthy' show sameness in that both relate to the health of the body, yet both are also different in that one signifies an object that is the cause of health, and the other signifies its manifestation. Analogical predication also occurs when, for example, the term 'healthy' is used of medicine and the human body in that the former is proportionate, and indeed causally responsible for this particular property in the latter.

Now, it is in the second sense of analogical predication that Aquinas is primarily interested, because it is in this sense that human beings are able to talk meaningfully about God. According to this mode of predication, humans are proportioned to God as creatures to creator. As mentioned, we only know anything about God from creatures. Aquinas is an empiricist. He thinks that all of our knowledge of *anything* begins with sense-experience. Any knowledge we have of God is going to start with some observable feature of the external world from which we can make inferences about God. And one of the inferences we are able to make about God is that he is the efficient cause of his creatures, which means that the latter participate to some degree in the divine essence. Accordingly, those perfections found in humans – such as being, goodness and wisdom – are therefore said to 'pre-exist' (*praeexistunt*) in God and, indeed, to do so in an excellent way (*excellenter*).[44]

According to the foregoing mode of predication, then, while we might say that Solomon is wise by virtue of possessing a human form of wisdom, we can infer that God, by contrast, is wise in a much more excellent way. And this does not mean that we are using the term 'wise' in two different, equivocal senses. Nor does it mean that we are using it univocally, for to do so would be to assume that God and creatures belonged to the same class, which is impossible given that essence and existence are distinct with respect to humans, whereas they are one and the same with respect to God. Rather, we understand pure perfections to exist in God because he is the efficient cause of creatures and of their perfections, and must therefore possess them – although in what mode we cannot entirely comprehend.

ACTUALITY AND POTENTIALITY

The most fundamental distinction in Aquinas's metaphysics is arguably that between act (*actus*) and potency (*potentia*) or between the possibilities inherent within things, and their realizations. Not only is this distinction fundamental to Aquinas's metaphysics, it cuts across his entire worldview. This is because Aquinas holds a teleological view of the universe according to which a thing's end (Gr. *telos*) is intimately bound up with its perfection. It is difficult if not impossible, for example, to understand Aquinas's ethics unless we understand that the human good consists in the actualization of certain capacities inherent in man. Likewise, we will utterly fail to understand Thomas's philosophical anthropology unless we appreciate that the soul, for him, is the actualization of the body. Nor will it be possible to understand his theory of cognition unless we appreciate that knowledge, on Thomas's account, is the actualization of a potentiality for apprehending abstract, universal concepts. Finally, we will fail to appreciate the need to affirm the existence of God unless we appreciate that he is required as the explanatory principle without which we cannot account for the existence of certain features of the external world, such as change, contingent being and so on.

Now, anyone familiar with Aristotle's philosophical worldview will notice at once its similarities with the above description. However, Aquinas adds a further metaphysical distinction to his largely Aristotelian metaphysics that changes the entire emphasis of his worldview as compared to that of Aristotle. We are referring, of course, to the distinction that Aquinas draws between essence (*essentia*) and existence (*esse*), which he inherits from Islamic philosophers such as Ibn Sīnā. But to see why any of this is important or original to Aquinas we need to back up a bit, as it were, and examine how he conceives of the basic furniture of the world.

Aquinas thinks that the first object that is apprehended or conceived by rational creatures is 'being' (*ens*).[45] Naturally, for such an object to be apprehended by the intellect, an ability to abstract its defining characteristics must become operational. And this ability for abstract thought is obviously tied to the acquisition of language. Prior such an acquisition, what we obviously encounter in a primitive sense when we experience the world is *beings*. Although young children, not to mention infants, are incapable of verbalizing anything in a coherent sense, they nonetheless start to realize differences between things that they will later come to call 'cats', 'dogs', 'chairs', 'people' and other such entities. Aquinas calls such entities 'substances' (*substantiae*) and they comprise, as it were, the furniture of the world.

For Aquinas, a substance is that which exists in its own right: it is a discrete thing in the world. As Aquinas puts it, the name substance 'signifies an essence to which it belongs to exist in the following way, that is, to exist per se.'[46] A substance, then, is something that exists 'through itself' or per se. Thus my dog Jasper is a substance, as am I. But to say that a substance is something that exists of or through itself should not be taken to mean that substances are causes of their own existence. Indeed, I am clearly not the cause of my own existence nor, for that matter, is Jasper. Rather, each of us is a substance in the sense that we both have a metaphysical core that persists through, and acts as a subject for, all of the modifications that we undergo throughout life. Thus, although Jasper's muzzle will start to become grey over time, she is nonetheless substantially the same dog as when she was younger, that is, prior to having acquired such a modification.

Aquinas calls these attributes 'accidents' (*accidentes*): modifications that do not, and indeed cannot, exist on their own. Rather, they must inhere in substances. He writes, 'That which is outside of the substance of a thing, and yet belongs to that thing, is called its accident.'[47] Thus, my height, weight and the colour of my hair, not to mention my location, are examples of accidents that modify the underlying substance that is me.

Notice that when my hair falls out or goes grey, or when I gain weight, these are examples of what Aquinas would call 'accidental change'. I might have changed in certain superficial ways, but I am still substantially the same being. Likewise, when Bob travels to Paris for a holiday, he may be said to change inasmuch as he is no longer in the location in which he ordinarily lives and works. Nonetheless, no one would accuse him of having become a completely different substance as a result: obviously he is still human. He changes places once he arrives in Paris, but this is merely a superficial or accidental modification. When Bob dies, however, and decomposes, that is a different matter. For then, Aquinas would say, he undergoes a process of 'substantial change.' He is no longer human per se, because the substance that was formerly Bob can no longer reason, love, play cards or indeed do any of the other activities that made him a member of the species *homo sapiens*. Rather, he has become an entirely different substance.

In order to undergo alteration in the ways just described, a substance must have elements of both finitude and permanence. That is, the substance must first have a beginning if not an end. It must also be one that is possessed of a metaphysical core, as it were, that sometimes persists through change with respect to its attributes (and therefore possesses some degree of permanence) and sometimes does not (due to its finitude). But what accounts for why it is that some forms of change allow the metaphysical core to persist, while other types of change involve a wholesale transformation of the substance? Why is Bob still fundamentally human when he goes grey, but substantially different when he dies and decomposes? Aquinas thinks that the answer lies in the fact that corporeal substances such as humans, dogs and trees are hylomorphic beings: composites of substantial form and prime matter.

The best way to understand the foregoing distinction is to continue with our example of substantial change. After Bob dies and his body has completely decomposed, we obviously no longer refer to him as 'human.' Still, Bob does not simply vanish. Even if *he* no longer exists as a material substance, there is at least *something* left of what was once Bob, even if that something does not contain any 'humanness' about it. Aquinas calls this prime matter (*prima materia*), and he regards it as pure potentiality that is capable of taking on different 'forms' (*formae*), the combination of which will comprise an individual substance of a definable nature that exists in the world.[48]

All material substances, then, are hylomorphic. In a purely abstract sense, matter is simply potential and, as such, cannot exist on its own. In the very materialistic culture that is the modern west, this sounds odd. Surely if anything actually exists, many will be tempted to say, it is matter. However, by saying that matter does not exist on its own, Aquinas is not suggesting that the material world is somehow unreal or conjured up by the imagination. Rather, he is simply saying that there is no such thing as matter that is not informed by some organizing principle that makes the product of such a composition a being of a certain class. Prime matter, in other words, is just a theoretical abstraction that Aquinas posits in order to explain the substrate which persists through substantial change. Form, on the other hand, is that which accounts for *why* some particular mass of matter is organized the way it is, and is thus capable of doing certain things and not others. According to Aquinas, then, there only exist individual substances, which are composites of matter and form: '. . . in things composed of matter and form, neither the matter nor the form nor even being *itself* can be called 'that-which-is.' Yet the form can be called "that-by-which-it is" insofar as [the form] is the principle of being. However, the whole substance itself is that-which-is'.[49]

How do we apprehend such principles if we do not have direct access to them, if we cannot, that is, directly experience forms – which are immaterial – and prime matter, which is not a substance, but mere potentiality? For Thomas, the answer is simple: we know the form or the organizing principle of a substance by its activities. A substance that can laugh, reason, learn foreign languages and do physical activities has the form of 'human-ness.' A substance that can take nourishment, reproduce and possesses within itself the ability to become an oak tree possesses the form of 'acorn-ness.' In the case of prime matter, we do not so much apprehend it by its capacities or activities as know it as the underlying, persisting principle of substantial change which accounts for why, to take an example, the caterpillar is able to become a butterfly.

Now, all of these examples pertaining to matter and substantial form are just specific examples of the more general and fundamental Aristotelian distinction between actuality and potentiality. Matter, as we have seen, is pure potentiality, while form supplies the principle that actualizes matter and places the emergent substance in a general class. Why, then, posit a difference between actuality and potentiality, and form and matter? Because the hylomorphic distinction applies, for Aquinas, solely to material substances. As we suggested a moment ago, many moderns might think that corporeal substances are all there *is* to external reality. But Aquinas disagrees. According to him there are substances that are in no way composed of anything material, and yet which can change: separated substances or angels. And since they can change, then they must have potentialities – such as the ability to think and to will – which have the ability to be actualized.

The distinction between actuality and potentiality, unlike the hylo-morphic distinction, then, can be found in the entire created order, that is, in everything other than God, and is a mark of their finitude and contingency. To say that the acorn is able to undergo a substan-tial change and become an oak tree is really just to say that it is an *actual* acorn that has the *potential* to become an oak tree. To say that the caterpillar is able to undergo a substantial change and become a butterfly is just to say that, while it is *actually* a caterpillar, it has the *potential* to become a butterfly. Finally, to say that an angel has the ability to elicit will-act y just means that, although he is *actually* willing x at T_1, he has the *potential* to will y at T_2. Any substance, for Thomas, that is capable of change is, so to speak, part act and part potency. It is in act to the extent that it itself or some power it possesses already exists or is perfected, and in potency to the extent that it itself or one of its powers has the capacity to be realized. As Aquinas puts it, 'that which can exist, but does not, is said to be in potentiality. That which now exists is said to be in actuality'.[50]

Much of the foregoing discussion justifies the assumption that Aquinas was deeply indebted to Aristotle for much of his meta-physics. The various distinctions between substance and accident, matter and form, and act and potency all have their sources in Aristotle, and they point to a teleological understanding of nature that both Aquinas and Aristotle shared. But, as mentioned at the outset, there is a final and crucial distinction that Aquinas is famous for developing and that he did *not* inherit from Aristotle, but rather from Ibn Sīnā: his defense of an objective distinction between essence (*essentia*) and existence (*esse*) in creatures.

Through his reading of Islamic philosophers such as Ibn Sīnā, Aquinas noticed that, although form or essence is related to matter as its actualizing principle, nonetheless a form or essence *in turn* stands in potentiality to something else, namely, existence.[51] Aquinas's great innovation over Ibn Sīnā was that, while he adopted this distinction, he rejected the latter's claim that existence and essence are distinct in the sense that the former is an *accident* of the latter. Rather, according to Thomas, existence is the metaphysical presupposition upon which accidents *themselves* are possible.[52]

What, then, is an essence according to Aquinas? It is that which *defines* a thing. Aquinas and his Latin-speaking contemporaries had a fitting philosophical synonym for this: *quidditas* or 'whatness'. To know the essence of something, so Thomas thought, is to know *what* it is. It is, in short, the nature of the thing made intelligible. In hylomorphic beings, the essence of the thing is just a way of restating the thing's substance, so that the essence of man, for example, will be defined as a rational, embodied being.

> Essence, properly speaking, is that which is signified through definition (*definitio*). Definition, however, embraces the principles of the species, but not the individual principles. Hence, in things composed of matter and form, the essence signifies not only the form, nor the matter alone, but the composite of matter and substantial form insofar as they are the principles of the species.[53]

By contrast, *esse* is the metaphysical act by which an essence or substance exists. Just as form is related to matter as act to potentiality, so existence stands to essence in a similar fashion. As Aquinas says: 'Existence signifies a certain act; for a thing is not said to exist because it is in potentiality, but because it is in act.'[54]

What is the point of this distinction? In part, it is simply a recognition of ordinary linguistic usage, which allows for a conceptual differentiation between *what* a thing is, and *whether* it is – a distinction, that is, between a being's essence and its existence. Most rational adults are quite capable of conceptualizing the nature of something, say *x*, without considering whether *x* exists in the outside world. Indeed, one might say that they are capable of conceptualizing it *despite* the fact that *x* might not exist in the outside world. As Aquinas says, 'I can know, for instance, what a man or a phoenix is and still be ignorant whether it has being in reality. From this it is clear that being is other than essence or quiddity.'[55]

However, what is really motivating Aquinas's embrace of this distinction is arguably much deeper than a mere exercise in linguistic analysis, and it seems to follow from his conception of God. Recall that in the Second and Third Ways, Aquinas claimed to demonstrate that God is Pure Actuality and Necessary Being. These proofs were rooted in the notion that contingent beings, by definition, must have a cause for their existence outside their natures since it is impossible for such beings to bring themselves into existence. In order to explain the ultimate existence of such creatures, there must therefore exist, so Thomas thought, a being in which no distinction could be drawn between its essence and its existence. For Thomas, in other words, there must exist a being whose essence just *is* its existence and therefore provides the ultimate ground of being for every finite creature, whether composed of matter and form or separate from matter.[56]

The distinction between essence and existence is therefore crucial to Aquinas's metaphysics, and points to a vital difference between his conception of the scope and nature of being, and that of Aristotle. For Aquinas there is a radical ontological dependence of creatures on a personal creator in a way that is simply not emphasized or even affirmed in Aristotle's thought. And in any case, whatever Aristotle's attitude towards the importance of God as an explanatory principle, he obviously had nothing like the *Christian* conception of God such as one finds in Aquinas. Thomas's metaphysics, then, as influenced as it was by Aristotle, starts with God, and ends with him, which should not really surprise us since Aquinas was first and foremost a theologian.

CHAPTER 3

PSYCHOLOGY

While we moderns commonly think of psychology as a science of the human mind, for Aquinas it is part of philosophy, and specifically the philosophy of nature. As we saw in Chapter 2, Aquinas thinks of natural things as forms united to matter or matter that is 'formed'. When he turns from inanimate natural substances to things that are alive, he follows Aristotle by thinking of the soul as the form that is united to, and organizes a matter we call the 'body'. Psychology for Aquinas, then, is the philosophical study of the soul (*anima*), which he regards as the actualizing principle of living things. The soul, however, is arguably so archaic a concept for many moderns that it warrants explanation. In this chapter we will try to explain what the soul is supposed to be, what powers it has, and whether it can still exist once its body dies.

THE ESSENCE OF THE SOUL

Fundamentally, Aquinas relies on the soul to explain why some things are alive, while others are not. Now consider what follows from this. First, all living things – from plants to animals to human beings – have souls. However, souls come in types or degrees. Plant souls have only the power to take nourishment and grow. For this reason, they are called 'vegetative' or 'nutritive' souls. Animal souls, by contrast, add the power of sensation, and so are called 'sensory' souls. The human soul alone displays the power of thought, and is therefore called the 'rational' soul. The higher types of soul include the lower types, along with their powers. Hence, although human beings specifically have rational souls, they also possess the powers associated with nutritive and sensory souls. After all, human beings grow and perceive no less than plants and animals do. Now, two powers stand out as especially important in the rational, or human, soul: the power of thought, which is a function of intellect (*intellectus*) and the power of choice, which is primarily a function of will (*voluntas*). We will return to these in more detail below. We must first elaborate on how Aquinas understands the nature of the human soul.

According to Aquinas, the rational soul has a unique, twofold nature: it is both the *substantial form* of the body to which it is united, and also a *subsistent form* in its own right. In its role as substantial form, the rational soul unites with, and is therefore closely tied to, the human body. Together, soul and body comprise a complete human being. As a subsistent form, however, the rational soul also has the power to exist apart from its body. In trying to reconcile these two formal descriptions of the soul, Aquinas enters hazardous philosophical terrain. For while we might allow that the soul can *either* inform the body *or* exist apart from the body, it is hard to see how it can do both, even at different times – unless it somehow changed its nature. It is as though Aquinas aims to combine two classical positions usually thought to be mutually exclusive: Plato's belief in the immortality of the soul and Aristotle's belief in the unity of soul and body. Put otherwise, Aquinas seems to face a dilemma: either the soul is closely bound up with the body as its form, as Aristotle thinks, and is therefore unlikely to survive its physical death, or it *can* survive the death of body, as Plato thinks, but is a wholly different substance from the body. But in the latter case it is hard to see how such an immaterial substance as the soul can have anything to do with a physical substance such as the body. That Aquinas offered a plausible solution to this dilemma is arguably one of his greatest achievements.

While Aquinas appears to assume that there is soul in all living things, some today might wonder whether we ought to follow Aquinas in positing a soul at all. This is because the ancient and medieval concept of soul seems to have been replaced for modern philosophers by the concept of *mind*, which in turn is typically reduced to the brain in contemporary discussions. The latter view is a consequence, of course, of the dominant materialist or 'physicalist' orientation of much contemporary philosophy of mind. So we really have two questions: (1) What exactly *is* the soul, on Aquinas's view? and (2) Why should we suppose that it actually exists? Now, while it might be tempting to argue for the soul's existence before taking up its essence, in this case knowing what the soul *is* should shed much light on why Aquinas thinks that it must exist.

In stating his view of what the soul is, Aquinas's first concern is to refute the materialist interpretation. From as far back as the pre-Socratics (6th–5th c. BC) to the present day, many philosophers have defended the claim that the soul, if it exists, must be 'some sort of body', as Aquinas puts it.[1] In recounting the materialist position, Aquinas notes two arguments that seem to support the claim that the soul must be a body or a physical substance. The first argument is based on motion. If the soul is the cause of the body's movement, as everyone agrees that it is, then it must have *contact* with the body. But if the soul has contact with the body, then it would have to *be* a body. If this is the case, then the soul will be a 'moved mover' (*movens motum*). Since all such principles are bodies, it will follow that the soul itself must be a material substance. The second argument considers the nature of knowledge. If knowledge is achieved by likeness to the thing known – as Aquinas thinks it is – then to the extent that the soul knows bodies, it must itself be a body. As we will see more fully in Chapter 4, the rational soul is capable of knowing every sort of material thing, or body, that there is. So how can it not be a body?[2]

In keeping with the scholastic method, Aquinas responds to these two arguments with his own counter-arguments. Now, for Aquinas, there *must* be a primary source of life to explain why some material substances are alive and capable of various activities. Aquinas calls this the soul. Assuming that everyone agrees that there must be *some* such principle in order to account for the distinction between living and non-living beings, the question then becomes whether it is a material or non-material principle. Aquinas's main quarrel with the materialist position is that if the soul is a physical body, then it cannot be the *first* principle of life, since all physical principles are by definition moved movers. Therefore, if the soul does in fact exist, then it is reasonable to expect it to be a necessary part of the human being, although *not* one of its body parts. Aquinas's basic argument, in syllogistic form, looks like this:

(P1) The soul is the first principle of life.
(P2) No body can be the first principle of life.
(P3) Therefore, the soul cannot be a body.

It is, of course, P2 that requires explanation. Now, Aquinas does not disagree per se with the notion that bodily organs can be principles of vital action. For example, as Aquinas concedes, the eye is the principle of vision, and the heart is a principle to the animal as a whole. Rather, his point is that no such physical principle can be the *first* principle of life. For example, the heart by itself is not a living thing, nor for that matter is the eye. If a body just by virtue of being a physical body could be a living thing, so Aquinas argues, then *all* bodies would be living. Since this is not the case, there must be some non-material actualizing principle that makes some bodies alive. It is this formal, actualizing principle, which Aquinas – following Aristotle and others – calls the 'soul'.

Now that the soul's essence has been defined in terms of its function of actualizing the body, we can attempt to explain more precisely how the soul and the body make up an individual person. Since Aquinas holds that these two distinct principles together constitute the human being, it may seem that he must be a mind-body dualist – a problematic position because of its apparent inability to explain the interaction between the mind and the body.

A good test case for whether or not Aquinas endorses mind–body dualism presents itself when Aquinas considers the issue of whether the soul should be strictly identified with the human being, a view Aquinas closely associates with Plato (*ca.* 428–347 BC). While we know far more about Plato's thought than Aquinas did, Plato is still generally considered the most famous dualist of the ancient world. As Aquinas understands this approach, the human being is characterized as essentially the soul merely using or even wearing a body. On this view, of course, the body in no way plays an essential part in what it means to be a human being. Aquinas, however, finds this view implausible, for two reasons. The first is that the definition of 'human being' includes matter as well as form.[3] But matter can only belong to the body. So, Aquinas thinks, the concept of a human being must include a body. Secondly, the soul cannot perform on its own all of the functions of a human being, since activities such as sensory perception, locomotion and visceral desire (hunger, thirst, sexual appetite) obviously rely on the presence of the body. We cannot see, for example, without using our eyes, run without using our legs, or take nourishment without using our stomachs. This is not to say that the soul does not have a crucial role to play in all such activities; only that, in this life, it must rely on the physical body for such operations.

Another reason why one might mistake Aquinas for being a dualist arises from his contention that the soul is subsistent – that is, that it can exist by itself apart from the body. Now, this seems to contradict the point just noted, that a soul separated from its body cannot perceive anything through its bodily senses. Without a body, there would be no need for the functions of growth, nutrition, reproduction or movement. And without any activity to ascribe to the soul, it would make no sense to suppose that the soul exists. The only function not obviously eliminated from a disembodied soul's repertoire is the rational function of thinking, if that can be done apart from a bodily organ. But how can a soul think without its brain?

As we have seen, Aquinas argues that the soul cannot itself be a body. Accordingly, he must now explain not only why the intellectual power of the soul is not a body, but also why it cannot even act *through* a bodily organ, unlike the sense powers. To do this he appeals boldly to the intellect's ability to know the natures of all material things, which would not be possible, so Aquinas thinks, if the intellect contained matter of any kind, 'because that which is in it naturally would impede the knowledge of anything else'.[4] That the intellect can take on the forms of all material things without distortion means that it cannot itself be made of matter, as is clearly the case with the brain. So the mind or intellect cannot be the brain. For the same reason, though, the mind cannot act through a bodily organ, as seeing, for example, acts through the eye. For if this were the case, the mind would be limited to knowing only those things that corresponded to what its organ (the brain) included, much as clear liquid poured into a coloured glass looks like the colour of the glass.[5] In other words, a mind that can know all things of a certain nature cannot share in that nature, or be limited by anything that shares in that nature.

Now the fact that the soul is capable of subsistence does not entail that in this life it exists or functions apart from the body. Rather, it means that the soul *can* exist outside of its union with the body and *will* do so once the body dies. But this prospect is enough to raise the specter of dualism again. Even René Descartes (1596–1650) – whose name is virtually synonymous with mind–body dualism among philosophers today – admits that the soul and body form a unity in our present state, even though mind and body have totally different natures.[6] Things are quite different from Aquinas's point of view. Despite the subsistence of the intellectual soul, it is united to a body as its form. We are back to the point from which we began, with the soul being the form, and actuality, of the body. And though (like Descartes) Aquinas thinks the soul can exist without the body, its separate existence is incomplete and imperfect – a worse state than its embodied existence. Yet it is easier to see this point when it comes to the bodily powers of soul like growing, moving and even sensing, than with the power of thinking. It may even seem that Aquinas is caught in a contradiction here: if the intellect (as Aquinas likes to call the mind) does not operate through a bodily organ, how can it possibly be the form of the whole body?

Here we must remember that forms can be related to matter in various ways. Some forms are just shapes that matter takes on, like the form of a statue representing Julius Caesar. In living things, the form of an organism will be its soul, which not only determines its outer shape, but also causes the thing to be alive. Aquinas describes subrational souls as completely 'immersed' (*immersa*) in the matter to which they are joined, by which he means that their functioning does not transcend their bodily organs.[7] This is the case (in varying degrees, Aquinas thinks) with all of our five senses. As Aquinas puts it, the actualization of the sense power just *is* the functioning of the sense organ. Thinking – the activity of the intellect – is different, however, for a number of reasons. One of these is that the intellect can think about itself while it is in the act of thinking, in a way that, for example, the eye cannot directly see itself, and still less see itself in the act of seeing. We are aware that we are seeing when we are doing so, of course, though such self-reflexivity is not a function of any of the five senses per se. Rather, it is the work of some 'common sense power' (*sensus communis*) to which the five senses direct their information.

When he wants to show that the intellect must be the form of the human body, Aquinas appeals to our self-awareness in a special way. The act of thinking is individual to each of us, 'for everyone is conscious that it is he himself who understands.'[8] Now, thinking is hardly something accidental to us, since it clearly distinguishes us from all of the other animal species. We would likely have doubts about the humanity of anyone who could not think or understand at all in the way that we do.

Given that thinking is an essential feature of human beings, then, we might still ask whether it is only some part of us that does the thinking, or whether it is the whole of us. Aquinas responds that our self-awareness shows that thinking is connected to sensing, since as Aquinas notes, 'it is one and the same man who is conscious both that he understands, and that he senses.'[9] But we cannot sense without a body, inasmuch as the sense powers operate through bodily organs. We are therefore forced to conclude that our intellect is part of us, and that it is somehow united to our body as its form.

These themes are among the most difficult in Aquinas's philosophical thought, so we will recap them before moving on. Psychology is the study of the soul, which for Aquinas is the explanatory principle for why some things are alive, and why they have the powers that they do. In living things there are various types of soul, which explains the gradations of life from plants to animals to human beings. The human soul is at once the most complex and powerful of all living forms. On the one hand, it contains all the lower types of soul. On the other hand, it expresses itself in thought and choice, which allows it to transcend the matter in which it exists. You can, after all, think about anything material, as well as things that are immaterial (like God, angels, numbers), and things that do not exist (like unicorns), or even things that cannot exist (like square circles). Furthermore, many objects that one can think about, one can either desire or not desire. The exception to this is when the desire is natural in the strong sense. Our desire to live forever, for example, which seems fanciful to many people, is for Aquinas a natural desire in this sense, since it follows from our intellect's grasping the concept of existence apart from limitations of place and time. And since Aquinas presumes that no natural desire can be for something unattainable, it follows that the human soul is incorruptible – that is, that it will live forever.[10]

THE SOUL'S POWERS

Thanks to its various gradations, the human soul has a number of powers, but its two principal powers are intellect (*intellectus*) and will (*voluntas*). These are, so to speak, the most excellent or highest powers in the soul, so Aquinas thinks, because they allow humans to live in a way that transcends their animal natures, thus allowing them to participate in the divine nature in a way that is not possible for the lower creatures. Moreover, both can be fully self-reflexive – that is, they can turn their own activity back on themselves, as we noticed earlier in regard to intellect.[11] They are also closely linked together, since we can hardly desire or choose what we do not know at all, and whatever we know about something obviously shapes whether we find it desirable or not. So the intellect seems to take precedence over the will, inasmuch as it has to present the will with an object to respond to.

It is easy enough to illustrate this relative priority of intellect to will, but tricky to do so without presupposing an act of will. For example, suppose I am thinking of going on a vacation, but I do not know where I want to go. I can find out about various types of vacations and venues, which obviously presupposes a desire to do so. Aquinas thinks of this as an act of the will moving the intellect to gather information related to vacation planning. As soon as I learn about the most beautiful beaches in the world, my will may quickly follow by forming a desire to visit one of them. But even in this case, the priority of intellect to will turns out to be reciprocal, since the will is needed to move the intellect to think about vacations in the first place. Sometimes we consciously notice this happening, as when we have to will ourselves to think about something in order to understand it.

While intellect and will depend on each other in their functioning, they are nevertheless very different powers. First, intellect is a power of knowing and understanding, while the will is a power of desiring and choosing. We have noted that the intellect acts before the will, insofar as desire (which Aquinas calls 'appetite') follows apprehension.[12] Aquinas also points out that the two powers relate differently to their objects. Intellect seeks to take its objects into itself, while the will strives to go out of itself to attain its object. Both powers seek to become one with their objects, but in contrasting ways. This difference also reveals one respect in which the will can be considered superior to the intellect, though in other respects Aquinas considers the intellect superior to the will. We will return to this point after looking at each power in a little more detail.

In his thinking about intellect, Aquinas is heavily indebted to Aristotle, particularly his work *On the Soul* (*De anima*). Like Aristotle, Aquinas reaches the conclusion that the intellect is a power of the soul – and not the very essence of the soul – and a different kind of faculty from the sense powers. Intellect differs from the senses not only because it does not directly use a bodily organ as the senses do, but also because it relates differently to its object. Where the objects of the senses are individual perceptible things, the objects of the intellect are the concepts derived from universal essences of these things, which are produced by means of a complex process of abstraction.

We will save the full description of this process for Chapter 4. For now we will note simply that without intellect we would have no knowledge in the proper sense of the term. We would of course have perceptions of all sorts of things around us, as animals do, and evaluations of what those perceptions mean to us, and even the ability to respond to these things so as to achieve our needs and sustain ourselves. But a whole other dimension of our experience as we now know it would be missing: knowing *what* things are, and knowing that we know this.

Thus far, we have seen that Aquinas characterizes the intellect as an immaterial, cognitive power of the soul that abstracts from the individuality of things in order to grasp them in universal terms. But is the intellect active or passive? In other words, can it act without first being acted on? Like Aristotle, Aquinas holds that the intellect is passive in the most general sense, because in understanding we move from potentiality to actuality.[13] At this point we must recall how fundamental this distinction between potentiality and actuality is for Aquinas, which he employs in this context to explain the special process by which an intelligent being – a knower – becomes like the thing it knows. If the intellect of a knower can become like a thing it is to know, it is 'in potentiality', so Aquinas thinks, to being like that thing until the knowing process is complete – at which point it is *actually* like the thing it has come to know. Notice, however, that when the intellect becomes actually like the thing it knows, it obviously does not do so in a material sense. Rather, it takes on the form without the matter. This leads us into another difficult but insightful part of Aquinas's philosophy of mind: how the mind takes objects in the world into itself by means of perception and comes to know them. Again, we will have more to say about how this happens when we turn to Aquinas's theory of knowledge in the following chapter.

For the moment, we should note that Aquinas thinks of the human intellect as at first like a 'blank slate' (*tabula rasa*) on which nothing has yet been written, as Aristotle put it.[14] So while Aquinas makes the ambitious claim that the human intellect 'has an operation [i.e. knowing] extending to universal being',[15] he balances that by adding that the human intellect – unlike the divine intellect – begins in a state of potentiality towards everything intelligible, though actually knowing nothing. The human intellect is passive because it must receive something in order to be actualized, much as matter needs to receive form in order to be actualized. Our intellects do not begin in an already actualized state, nor can they actualize themselves. Indeed, self-actualization in this sense is a contradiction in terms for Aquinas, since – as we saw in Chapter 2 – nothing can be actual and potential at the same time and in the same respect.

So is the human intellect entirely passive, like the sense powers which merely receive sensible impressions (colours, sounds, smells, etc.) from things? That would be the case if the things around us were fully intelligible, or knowable, in themselves, and just waiting to encounter a knower to burst upon human consciousness. But while an apple can be actually red (or green), and needs only to be illumined in order for its colour to make an impression upon a waiting eye, Aquinas holds that the apple as a whole is only potentially intelligible. Once again, Aquinas follows Aristotle rather than Plato in thinking that the forms of natural things do not exist apart from matter. Yet like both ancient thinkers, he connects intelligibility – the ability of something to be understood – closely with immateriality. This may strike us as a strange equation, and not especially plausible. Immaterial things often seem to us much harder (if not impossible) to understand than material things. Yet when we think about material *things*, we are thinking of them as already formed in some way, and not just as indeterminate concatenations of matter. In Aquinas's terms, things are intelligible insofar as they are informed, for it is by their forms that we understand them. And forms, as we have seen already, are not material features of things (like arms and legs), but principles of actualization in things (like the soul in relation to a living being).

Since our minds are designed to know material things, which turn out not to be intelligible in their own right, the human intellect must also have an active power, specifically a 'power to make things actually intelligible'.[16] Following a long Aristotelian tradition, Aquinas will call this active power the 'agent intellect' (*intellectus agens*), while he will call the passive power that we described earlier the 'potential' or 'possible intellect' (*intellectus possibilis*).[17] Having established a need for an agent intellect, Aquinas can also resolve the further question that divided philosophers and theologians of his time about the agent intellect: is it a power in each of us, or is there a single agent intellect of which we all make use? If the agent intellect were a power separate from all individual souls, we would have to presume that there was only one such power on which all human minds relied to make things in the world intelligible. But if the agent intellect is a power *of* the soul, as Aquinas has argued, then there are as many agent intellects as there are souls, and as many souls are there are human beings.[18]

Now that we have examined the basic features of the intellect, we may turn to the will. Where we may tend to think of the will first and foremost as the power of choice, Aquinas thinks of the will first as an appetite – specifically an intellectual appetite, to distinguish it from sensual appetites. To say that will is an appetite means that it is a type of desire or inclination. Like all powers of the soul, the will has an object which, Aquinas thinks, is the good, just as the natural object of the intellect is truth. But if the will has a natural object that it cannot help but pursue, this may seem to compromise its freedom. For how can freedom and necessity co-exist within the will? Aquinas thinks this apparent contradiction can be resolved by distinguishing different senses of necessity. If you are physically compelled to do something by someone else, your doing that thing becomes necessary in a way that clearly is not compatible with your acting freely. Another type of necessity arises, by contrast, when you desire an end which you cannot attain by your own powers. For example, if you wish to make a journey across an ocean, you will need a ship or a plane to get you across.[19] In that case, you still remain free to desire to make the journey or not, so whatever necessary consequences emerge from that desire do not change the fact that the initial desire was not necessary – that is, it did not compel you to follow it. So such 'necessity of the end' does not contradict our freedom.

Now, Aquinas thinks that there is one end which is not chosen, but is necessary for all of us. If he is right to think of the will as an appetite, it is not so strange to expect there will be some object – the most final of all goals – which we naturally (and thus necessarily) desire. Nowadays we tend to think of appetites as being in some sense sub-rational; when we are hungry we cannot but desire food, for example. But our hunger, of course, is a physical desire, not a rational one. Aquinas, however, has no trouble thinking of an appetite existing at the rational level. Because will is a power of the rational soul, it can desire or incline towards its object in universal terms. And because will is an appetite, its desire for its object – which Aquinas characterizes as the universal good – is as natural and necessary to it as three angles are to a triangle.[20] This will be discussed in greater detail in Chapter 5 when we turn to happiness.

In sum, in every voluntary action, intellect and will cooperate. This holds true from the beginning of any human action when we are considering what to do, all the way to our decision to do it.[21] Inasmuch as the two powers interact in every choice, so Aquinas thinks, and neither power can act independently of the other, they are deeply interdependent for their respective operations. Nevertheless, Aquinas is sometimes described as an 'intellectualist', because he gives priority to intellect over will, as we saw earlier. This distinguishes him from 'voluntarists', who regard the will as the supreme power in us. Now, it is true that Aquinas holds that the intellect is a higher power than the will insofar as intellect has a more universal object – the natures of the good things we desire – than the will, which desires good things themselves.[22] So knowledge of material things is better than love of them. On the other hand, is it *really* better to know God than to love him? In answering this, Aquinas recalls that intellect and will relate to their objects in opposite ways: while intellect takes its object into itself, will goes out of itself to the object. Since God is greater in being and goodness than the human mind, it is better to reach out to God in love than to bring God into the confines of the mind. In such a case, then, will is superior to intellect, insofar as it is related to an object that is superior to the intellect. In the final analysis, however, intellect is unqualifiedly (*simpliciter*) superior because its objects, the forms of desirable goods, are more abstract than the objects of the will – the desirable objects *themselves* – which are mixed with matter.[23] Because its object is higher, then, Aquinas concludes that the intellect is in principle higher than the will, even though the will can be considered superior in some respects.

IMMORTALITY

A distinctive feature of Aquinas's thought is his belief that human beings have a natural desire to live forever, and it is difficult to quarrel with him over this. Indeed, it is a claim that appears to be firmly grounded in our experience. Most rational people do not want to die and will therefore, all things being equal, generally attempt to delay the inevitable for as long as they can. This shows, Aquinas thinks, that human beings have a natural desire for immortality. Now, we have spent some time exploring intellect and will as powers of the human soul, because for Aquinas they are its highest powers.

Those distinctions alone would warrant special attention. But there is another reason why Aquinas takes particular care with them: they provide the basis for his doctrine that the human soul is, in his terminology, 'subsistent' (*subsistens*) and 'incorruptible' (*incorruptibilis*).[24] When these two qualities are joined, the result is immortality. But just how good are the philosophical arguments for this claim? Some commentators on Aquinas suggest that the reasons that prompted him to defend the persistence of the soul after death are primarily religious.[25] After all, Aquinas was a Christian theologian who believed that God provides salvation to human beings through Jesus Christ, yet salvation thus understood requires that we exist beyond our natural death. Now while Aquinas clearly takes this matter on faith, it does not prevent him from thinking that there are also good philosophical *reasons* for supposing that the soul is immortal – even if these reasons may be prompted by his religious convictions.

Before we turn to the reasons he gives for personal immortality, though, we should notice that Aquinas is in a potentially perilous position. This is because, as we noted earlier, if the soul is the substantial form of the body, then it runs counter to the natural relationship of matter and form to suppose that the latter can exist apart from the former. So, the soul as substantial form does not seem a good candidate for immortality. This may seem easily solved by referring back to the soul as a subsistent form, since subsistent forms by definition can exist by themselves, without depending on anything else. In this case, my soul would guarantee my immortality, if my soul is identical to me. But, as we have seen, Aquinas clearly thinks that a human soul is not same thing as a human being. In one of his biblical commentaries, he even says explicitly, 'My soul is not I.'[26]

The question of human immortality, then, involves for Aquinas explaining both how the human soul, which is a part of us, can survive unharmed despite the bodily death of a person, while also explaining how the soul, once separated from the body, can be reunited to it in such a way as to reconstitute a human being. We have already seen how Aquinas argues that the human soul is incorporeal and subsistent – that is, how it can exist in its own right without depending on anything else to continue existing.[27] This may seem to imply that a subsistent soul will also be immortal. But the soul's capacity to exist apart from the body in and of itself does not guarantee that it has the capacity to exist forever. For example, it might wear out after a sufficiently long period, as all bodies do. Like bodies, the soul too came into being at some point, so why should we not think that it will likewise cease to be at some point? And, finally, what exactly is the soul supposed to be doing while it exists by itself, without the body through which it accomplishes most everything it does? Even thinking, as Aquinas describes it, requires the use of images in the brain, even if it is not the brain itself that thinks.[28]

In answering the question of whether the soul is immortal Aquinas points out that the human soul cannot be destroyed by the death of the body if it is a subsistent form. This is because a subsistent form has being in its own right, and cannot be corrupted by anything that is not essential to it.[29] Now Aquinas regards the soul not only as a subsistent form but also a simple form. For this reason he was careful to distinguish intellect and will as powers or capacities of the rational soul, and not different essences of the soul.[30] All corruption, as Aquinas thinks of it, occurs when something that is composed, or put together, falls apart. But in the case of a form like the soul, which is simple (i.e. non-composite), there are no parts which, once put together, can come apart. As Aquinas says, 'it is impossible for a form to be separated from itself.'[31] Now it may seem that Aquinas is arguing in circles here. But from his point of view he is simply drawing out the implications of what has already been established. First, recall, he classified the soul as a form that actualizes a certain kind of matter. He then argued that a soul endowed with rational power can perform acts in which the body has no share. But a soul that can perform its own action without the help or involvement of the body has to be subsistent. In other words, if it can act on its own, so Aquinas argues, then it must be able to exist on its own.

Aquinas, however, goes even further than this: he says that it is 'impossible' for the human soul to be corruptible.[32] Having explained how the soul – if it is a form and a subsistent form at that – is immortal, Aquinas must address the question of what exactly the soul will do after its separation from the body, and *how* it will do it. Without its body, the soul will not be able to perform any of the functions it did when alive, except perhaps for the activity of thinking. Aristotle had speculated that if the soul had an activity that it could do all by itself, it might be able to engage in that activity even if it were apart from the body.[33] Aristotle concluded that this would be the activity of thinking, and Aquinas agrees. But even thinking poses potential problems for a soul that is separated from the material body since, on Aquinas's Aristotelian account, human thought always involves images (*phantasmata*),and images rely for their existence on a corporeal organ, namely the brain.[34]

The separated soul, then, poses a real problem for Aquinas, which arises from the tension we noticed between the soul's two 'formalities': substantial form and subsistent form. For some, the separated soul illustrates the contradiction between these two descriptions of soul. There is only one activity, it seems, that the separated soul and the embodied soul can share in, but the conditions under which the soul thinks in both cases are markedly different. Aquinas proposes to resolve this difficulty by making some distinctions. First, we must distinguish between the soul's nature and its mode of being. Understanding through images is part of the soul's nature for Aquinas, and fits well with its embodied mode of being. The problem of disembodied understanding could be resolved if we were to suppose that the soul's embodiment was somehow unnatural or accidental to it. But for Aquinas this would undermine the very rationale for the soul's union with the body. If the soul could perform its noblest activities apart from the body, then the union of the two would be more for the good of the body than for the good of the soul: something that is, so Aquinas thinks, 'absurd' to believe.[35]

The resolution Aquinas proposes is that the soul, once separated from the body, enters into a new, and not strictly natural, mode of being. In this higher mode, which is better suited to disembodied creatures like angels, the human soul participates for a time, though its quality of understanding is inferior to that of angels. Nonetheless, this higher mode of understanding allows the separated soul to perform its activity without recourse to the images stored in the corporeal brain. As Aquinas puts it, the soul that is separated from the body possesses a mode of understanding that permits it to turn to 'simply intelligible objects, as is proper to other separate substances'.[36] Because of the relative weakness of the human intellect, the comprehension that a separated soul has of these intelligibles will be imperfect and marked by confusion. A good analogy might be the kind of understanding that non-scientists have of the concepts of a specialized science like astrophysics.[37] Nonetheless, and somewhat paradoxically, even though embodied souls end up understanding in a mode that is inferior to that of angels, they are still better off than separated souls. This is because it is better for us to have 'perfect and proper' knowledge of sensible things through an inferior mode of cognition than to have 'confused and general' understanding through a more perfect form of knowing.[38] If God had wanted to make human understanding like that of the angels, he would either have had to make human beings into angels (which would have eliminated a gradation in the universe, thus diminishing its perfection), or settle for making human minds that operate in a non-abstractive mode and never reach perfect understanding.

Aquinas therefore finds a way to explain how the soul can continue to exist apart from the body, as well as engage in the activity of thinking – albeit a strange and imperfect kind of thinking. This mode of being is imperfect for the soul in two ways: first its activity is not perfect because it is deprived of the body through which it naturally acts, whose organs allow it to attain perfect functioning, even at its highest mental level. Second, as an imperfect mode of existence, the separated state does not bring the soul to fulfilment, and so it is only temporary. The problem is that, although Aquinas's arguments for the separated state are able to provide an account of survival, they are inadequate to provide a proper foundation for immortality, which requires a permanently deathless state. In order to attain the happiness for which we are intended, in other words, the soul must be rejoined with the body, and the reconstituted person placed in a right relationship with God. As one might suspect, this will require not merely the culmination of natural forces, but some special action on God's part.

In explaining the disembodied survival of the soul, then, Aquinas clearly relies on philosophical reasoning to a great extent. However, human immortality and beatitude cannot, so Aquinas thinks, be explained in philosophical terms alone. And while we cannot offer a complete theological account of Aquinas's views on post-mortal existence, it is necessary to point out that, for Aquinas, salvation requires the resurrection of the body and its reunion with the soul. Now the resurrection of the body is of course a vital teaching of Christian eschatology – or theory of last things – and is based on the belief that Christ, after his crucifixion, was raised from the dead. While Aquinas believes that all who have died must undergo resurrection in the manner of Christ if they are to achieve eternal life, he also has philosophical reasons for insisting that resurrection is necessary for ultimate human happiness. This follows from the naturalness of the union of soul-as-form with the body as its matter. As Aquinas sees it, the soul has a natural aptitude for uniting with the body. Thus, while one's soul can exist apart from one's body, the former will be incomplete and unsatisfied unless and until it is reunited with the latter.[39] This is because if such reunion could *not* be achieved, then a natural desire would be frustrated – which (as we noted earlier) Aquinas sees as an impossibility. It is necessary, then, that the disembodied soul rejoin its body in order for us to achieve fulfilment and attain beatitude in the vision of God.

Finally, Aquinas is adamant that the body with which the soul is reunited must be the very same body it had while on earth; otherwise the resulting substance will not constitute the same person. Of course, it is necessary, if resurrection is to occur, that the rational soul be united again with *some* body, which is to say, a body 'of the same nature and species as was the body laid down by the soul at death'.[40] The foregoing statement is not meant to imply that personal immortality can be achieved merely by means of one's soul uniting with some generic human body. Indeed, the only way to achieve *individual* immortality, so Aquinas thinks, is for the selfsame soul to be reunited to the selfsame matter. Aquinas writes, 'Just as the same specific form ought to have the same specific matter, so the same numerical form ought to have the same numerical matter . . . Therefore, since the rational soul that survives remains numerically the same, at the resurrection it must be reunited to numerically the same body.'[41] How can all of this possibly be achieved? Not by any natural process, Aquinas thinks, since nature can only preserve the species in face of the demise of the individual. Only a divine action – miraculous from our point of view – can restore one and the same individual to life.

CHAPTER 4

EPISTEMOLOGY

'Epistemology' is a modern term and so never appears in Aquinas's writings by that name, yet there can be little doubt that he offers a systematic account of knowledge (Gr. *epistēmē*).[1] Unlike much epistemology since Descartes (1596–1650), however, Aquinas's theory of knowledge is not concerned with refuting sceptical concerns about the possibility of certain knowledge, or the relationship between the mind and the world. Instead, his account provides something more like a description of the cognitive process: we come first to perceive things with our senses and then to know things with our intellect. Apart from the general problem of how we sometimes fall into error, Aquinas assumes that our cognitive powers are well designed for their job of decoding the world in which we find ourselves. Inspired as in other aspects of his thought by Aristotle, Aquinas begins his account of our knowledge with sensory perception. Yet, as in his metaphysics, he transforms Aristotle's approach to cognition by incorporating medieval innovations arising from both the later Aristotelian tradition and from Augustine's influence on later medieval thought. The resulting theory of knowledge not only attracted intense attention from later medieval thinkers, but also remains an intriguing alternative to the Cartesian epistemology that has bedevilled modern philosophy for so long.

PERCEPTION

All our knowledge begins with the senses, Aquinas thinks, and consequently his whole epistemology rests on sensory cognition as its foundation. The senses themselves do not provide us with knowledge, which is our ultimate goal, but rather with awareness of the material things around us. Aquinas makes a distinction between a reasoned understanding of things, which he calls scientific knowledge (*scientia*), and a mere awareness of them and their qualities, which he calls cognition (*cognitio*). This distinction, as we shall see, is fundamental to his epistemology.

Why does Aquinas deny that the senses can give us knowledge? It is not because he doubts that the objects we perceive are actually present, or that they possess the qualities they appear to have. Apart from special circumstances, as when we see an oar in water looking bent as a result of refraction, Aquinas is not mistrustful of the senses. When they are functioning normally, our senses report things in the world according to the impressions they make on us. Yet our five external senses – sight, hearing, smell, taste and touch – are subject to a number of limitations causing their cognition to fall short of the requirements of knowledge. Each of these senses has a 'proper object', which only *it* can detect, as only sight can detect colour. The converse is also true: colour is the only quality that sight can perceive. Since Aquinas believes that substances are not merely collections of accidental qualities like colour, texture, etc., the external senses cannot by themselves perceive any material object in its completeness. Knowledge, of course, requires total comprehension of its object; consequently, the external senses – since they grasp only accidental qualities of things – cannot provide knowledge as such. Indeed, for Aquinas an object can be grasped in its completeness only after it has passed through the external senses to the internal senses. We will outline this in further detail below.

In addition to identifying the accidental qualities of objects, the senses also perceive *individual* things, which Aquinas calls 'singulars'. Borrowing from Plato and Aristotle, Aquinas regards knowledge as being universal, immaterial and immutable.[2] But our sensory cognition cannot measure up to any of these stringent criteria. For example, when I see a car, how much can I know about it if I rely only on what my senses tell me? What I see is an individual thing that moves, has a specific colour, and makes sounds, yet when I identify it as a car, I must rely on universal terms like the concept of car or the word 'car'. Moreover, the car I see is material; if it were not, it would be imperceptible to my eyes. As a material thing, it is also subject to change: its parts will deteriorate; some will be replaced; and eventually it will no longer function as a car. Now, individuality, materiality and mutability all pose problems for knowledge, though not in the same way or to the same degree. Aquinas holds that individuality is intelligible, but materiality and mutability are not.[3] After taking a closer look at the object in front of me, I may say, 'That fast-moving red thing is a car.' In so doing, though, I am identifying an individual thing in universal terms, as what it is (a car). While this may seem to be a judgement made by the senses, Aquinas thinks that another faculty of the mind makes this determination. If the senses cannot perceive the whole individual object, still less can they perceive it in universal terms, according to its nature. As Aquinas puts it, the senses always relate to singulars.[4]

Although the senses do not provide knowledge, they inaugurate the cognitive process leading ultimately to knowledge of things. The process of moving from our first awareness of something to knowledge of it is a multi-stage process, which Aquinas describes in detail. Because it provides the basis for Aquinas's theory of knowledge, we will sketch the key moments in this process in what follows.

The path to knowledge, so Aquinas thinks, begins when one or more sense powers are affected, or 'altered' (*immutari*), by a sensible quality of a thing outside of oneself. When you see a red car, the redness of the car makes an impression on your eye. Your eye need not become red, in which case it would take on the quality as it exists in the object, as your hand is heated when you immerse it in hot water. Aquinas calls this latter kind of alteration in a sensitive organ 'natural alteration' (*immutatio naturalis*). But the key to sensory perception is found in 'spiritual alteration' (*immutatio spiritualis*), in which 'an intention of the sensible form is effected in the sense organ.'[5] In other words, when we perceive the qualities of things around us, certain forms of these objects – the colour of the car, the sound of its engine, etc. – are received into our sense organs. Once the alteration has taken place, these qualities come to reside in the sense powers, but in a new way: where they previously existed only in the material object, they now exist in the sense powers as *de-materialized* forms. This is not to say that they are immaterial, but only that they do not share in the matter of the original object. When Aquinas calls these sensory forms 'intentions' or 'species', he means that they are likenesses of the forms that exist in real things.

After these sensory qualities have made their various impressions on the knowing subject and have been converted into 'species', they need to be unified and made into a likeness of the complete object.

Otherwise, sight may tell us that the car is red, and touch that the hood is warm, and so on, but on this basis we will be unable to identify the car as a complete thing. In order to explain how the disparate data are assembled into the sensory likeness of the whole car, Aquinas posits another set of sense powers, the internal senses (*sensus interiores*).[6] Before the various impressions of the external senses can be collated, they need to be received into the power known as the 'common sense' (*sensus communis*). Once the sensory likenesses of the car are in the common sense power, it compares them and judges that, while different, they all belong to the same object.[7] The next step in the cognitive process is the production of a likeness of the complete, individual object. Aquinas calls this likeness the 'phantasm', retaining Aristotle's Greek term *phantasma* for the non-material but still individualized likeness of the individual thing we have perceived.[8] Sensory cognition for Aquinas culminates in the formation of the phantasm, which plays an essential role in our knowledge of material things.

It is worth pausing here to notice Aquinas's insistence that our knowledge of material things must derive from the things themselves. This may seem obvious to us, but in Aquinas's time, there were actually a number of competing explanations that had already been proposed and carried considerable philosophical weight. For example, the soul might know material things through its own essence; or through intelligible species innate in it from its creation; or through species derived from separate, Platonic forms; or it might know material things through the ideas God has of them.[9] Each of these explanations, however, short-circuits empirical knowledge by appealing to some higher (e.g. Platonic forms, divine Ideas) or prior (e.g. innate ideas) source of knowledge than the object we actually encounter. As Aquinas sees it, this involves explaining the obscure through the even more obscure, which is never his preference. Notwithstanding his theological convictions, he adopts an empiricist approach to knowledge: all knowledge arises from sense experience. If we need to grasp an individual thing in *universal* terms in order to know it, why should we seek this universality in a source outside our experience? Instead, Aquinas appeals to the power of the intellect itself to make things intelligible: the agent intellect, he says, 'causes the phantasms received from the senses to be actually intelligible by a process of abstraction'.[10]

INTELLECT AND KNOWLEDGE

An empirical theory of knowledge faces two obvious problems: first, how are we to find anything universal in the individual objects we perceive? Second, how can there be knowledge of anything non-material? As we saw in Chapter 3, there needs to be an agent intellect because material things are not already intelligible when we first perceive them. In terms of the potential/actual distinction in Chapter 2, material objects are only *potentially* intelligible as they exist in the world; in the process of our coming to know them, we make them *actually* intelligible. How does this happen? In perceiving the red car, our external senses disassemble (so to speak) the object into the different qualities that make an impression on each sense organ. After that, our internal senses and intellect then reassemble it: first, in the phantasm, which represents the complete individual object, and then in the intelligible species (*species intelligibilis*), which the agent intellect abstracts from the phantasm. The agent intellect performs the dual function of 'illuminating' the phantasm and abstracting the intelligible species from it.[11]

The terms 'illumination' and 'abstraction' may suggest that the agent intellect first shines a light on the sensory likeness of the thing, and then surgically removes the universal form of the thing, which merely lies hidden in the phantasm. Aquinas, however, characterizes the process in far less dramatic terms: 'This is what we mean by abstracting the universal from the particular, or the intelligible species from the phantasm: . . . considering the nature of the species apart from its individual qualities represented by the phantasms.'[12]

As in the case of the phantasm, Aquinas describes the intelligible species as a 'likeness' (*similitudo*), but unlike the phantasm the intelligible likeness is fully de-materialized and de-individualized, since it exists in the intellect. The intelligible species of the red car includes only the nature of car, and leaves aside all the individual conditions that pertain to *this* particular red car. It is this universal likeness that the agent intellect impresses upon the potential intellect.

It may seem that with the intelligible species in its sights, our intellect is finally in a position to *know* its object for what it is: a red car. But this would imply that the intelligible species is what the intellect understands. Here Aquinas is very careful to say that the intelligible species is 'the form *by which* the intellect understands' its real object: the natures of things in the world.[13] Indeed, Aquinas argues that if the intelligible species *were* the object that we know, knowledge of the world would be secondary to knowledge of our own minds – exactly the reverse of what he takes to be the case. While Aquinas makes this point unambiguously, it does not make his view easier to understand. For if we know the red car by means of an abstract likeness that represents it, it may seem that our knowledge of the object has to be mediated through the mental instruments (the phantasm and the intelligible species) we use to apprehend it. Even though Aquinas asserts a direct realist position when it comes to cognition, his description of the intelligible species as a 'likeness' opens the door to a representationalist interpretation.[14] This does not, however, raise for Aquinas the intractable question of how we can get from knowledge of our own mind's contents to knowledge of things in the world. Rather, he assumes that while our cognitive powers produce both the phantasm and intelligible species, there is no way for us to get these crucial steps wrong. For Aquinas as for Aristotle, you either apprehend something or you do not; anything less than perfect success means an outright failure of the intellect to grasp the thing.

The intelligible species is not the object we seek to know; consequently, the process of knowing an individual object is not yet complete. Even if we grasp the universal nature of the object, we are after all trying to know an individual thing. According to Aquinas, the intellect needs finally to turn back to the phantasms (*conversio ad phantasmata*) in order to understand the individual thing in the world.[15] Why should this be necessary? Up to now, there has been an inward and upward movement, from the red car to my sense powers of sight and hearing, from these external senses to my internal senses (the common sense and imagination), and then to my intellect. Why should the intellect turn back to lower sensory powers, as Aquinas thinks of them, to complete its intellectual cognition of the car?

We have already seen that Aquinas thinks that the intellect performs some acts independently of any sense powers – for example, abstraction of the intelligible species. But this point must not be taken too far. Aquinas understands equally well that the intellect relies on the sense powers for its activity. If the intellect operated entirely without any reliance on sensory powers, why would it be affected when the senses are impaired? Yet we know that a drunk person's judgement may be as much impaired as his motor control. Likewise, brain injuries can permanently alter a person's cognitive abilities, or cause loss of knowledge that the person once possessed.[16] Moreover, Aquinas cites the familiar practice of grasping a more remote universal by means of individual examples. If you are teaching a child to add, for instance, you might begin by setting out a row of building blocks from which the child can form mental images (phantasms); then she can move beyond merely counting the blocks to adding abstract quantities. While this is an elementary example, Aquinas thinks that this practice applies even to the highest levels of cognition, as when we try to cognize immaterial beings like angels and God. Since we have no phantasms of such beings, we are at a loss to conceive of them. We will consider Aquinas's remedy for such agnosticism about immaterial beings below. Yet if the senses did not play a necessary role in understanding before and after abstraction, this problem of understanding spiritual entities would not arise.

While these indications illustrate the dependence of the intellect on the senses when using the knowledge we have already acquired, Aquinas has more fundamental reasons to insist, as Aristotle did, that 'the soul understands nothing without a phantasm.'[17] For we are trying to know not only the nature that all cars share, but also *this* car: the red coupe right in front of me. This is how Aquinas thinks about the intellect's 'proper object': it is a 'nature or quiddity (*quidditas*) existing in corporeal matter', the universal nature in the individual thing.[18] Aquinas suggests a parallel between ourselves and material objects: inasmuch as our intellects are united to bodies, they are suited to knowing material things – which are like us in that they are constituted by forms united to matter. From this it follows that if we are to know the natures of these things accurately, we must know them as they exist in individual material things. As we have seen, the phantasm is the only likeness we have of the individual thing. So the intellect must turn to the phantasm in order to know how the universal is related to the individual thing before me.

Thus far, we have traced out the steps we go through when we come to know a material object. Aquinas calls this process 'intellectual apprehension'. Have we then attained knowledge of the red car? Yes and no. We have grasped the nature – the 'what it is' – of a thing that made an impression on our senses. We have connected that nature back to the object from which it came – the individual car. We also noted at least one quality of the car – its colour. And we formed the first propositions about it: 'That thing is a car' and 'That car is a red coupe.' With these statements, which Aquinas would call 'judgements', we can say that we know something about this object: what it is and what it is like in some small detail. There are, however, two caveats on our new claim to knowledge: first, our knowledge of the thing is far from complete; and second, as soon as we form a judgement about something in propositional form, we could be mistaken. If we are mistaken, then our claim to knowledge fails, of course, since 'false knowledge' is a contradiction in terms. Let us consider each of these concerns more closely.

As one would expect with an empiricist like Aquinas, our knowledge of things will not be instantaneous; rather, we come to know things gradually and incrementally by relating them to other things we already know. In the example we have been considering, we related the car to a type of car (a coupe), which is to say, a more general classification (*genus*) to a more specific one (*species*). This process could go on at some length adding more specifications: if the car is a coupe, what make and model is it? What size is its engine? And so on. Apart from learning more about it by classifying it more precisely, we can also inquire about its various qualities, and whether these are necessary to it or merely incidental. Aquinas would think of these as 'accidents', in terms of Aristotle's categories: quantity, quality, relation, activity, passivity, when, where, position and condition.[19] The car is either moving or not; it is either in good working condition or not; it has a certain market value at any given time; etc. To say the least, if all that we know about the car is that it is a red coupe, there is plenty of room for our knowledge to grow. Aquinas thinks of this as happening through a process of affirmations and negations (which he would call 'composition and division'), such as 'This car is (or is not) a Thunderbird.'

Our knowledge can grow by means of apprehending more about a thing, or by reasoning. As soon as we have two propositions related to each other, we can reason our way to a third proposition – the conclusion of the first two. If we know that the car is a Thunderbird, and that Ford makes the Thunderbird, then we know that this car is a Ford. Aquinas thinks of reasoning as the characteristic mode of operation for the human intellect. As abstraction is the key to apprehension, so reasoning is the key to knowledge for us. By reasoning our understanding grows, but it never reaches perfection, so Aquinas thinks. Perfect knowledge requires that we know everything about a thing or a kind of thing (a species or genus of things). While this is not logically impossible, it is practically impossible. Reasoning for us takes time and effort, and the limitations on our time, energy and motivation to learn mean that no individual will achieve perfect knowledge of any one thing, let alone of everything that can be known. Fortunately, knowledge is not an individual endeavor undertaken alone. There is a vast storehouse of human knowledge acquired over the course of recorded history to which we appeal whenever we individually learn something new. As Aquinas sees it, each of us goes through a process to perceive a thing and then grasp what it is. From our apprehension of the object we form a concept of it that is our own. But as soon as we express that concept in words, we move from the personal to the social sphere. The words we use are not our own, but they allow us both to express what we know and to tap into a body of knowledge shared by all human beings. At this point we may think of *scientia* in the more familiar sense of 'science': an organized body of knowledge established by the efforts of many contributors over time.[20] Aquinas does not believe that human knowledge as a whole can be perfected by comprehending all that is knowable. But suppose we narrow the focus down to how perfectly we may know any one thing.

What does it mean to know (*scire*) something? Like other medieval scholastics, Aquinas's thought about *scientia* is firmly rooted in Aristotle's *Posterior Analytics*, on which he wrote a commentary. There Aquinas writes:

[T]o know something in an unqualified sense is to know it perfectly. This means knowing the truth about it perfectly . . . Therefore, in order to know it perfectly, we must know the cause of the thing . . . [I]f we knew only the cause, we would not yet actually know the effect and, therefore, we would not know it in an unqualified way . . . [T]o know in an unqualified way, we must know the cause as *applied* to the effect.[21]

To return to our example of the car, perfect knowledge of the car would require that we know its cause, which is to say its four causes (its matter, form, maker and purpose), as well as its effects, which we might understand as everything the car is capable of doing. With respect to a manmade object like a car, it may seem that we can come close to understanding it as completely as *scientia* requires.

But two factors prohibit complete scientific knowledge of even a car. First, no artefact qualifies as a substance in Aristotle's terms, since its form is artificially imposed on its matter. Hence, to understand the car completely, we must know the matter out of which it is made, which has its own natural form. This brings us to a second problem: *scientia* requires that we reason from necessary propositions, those which cannot be otherwise than they are. To form necessary propositions about something, Aquinas thinks, we must know its essence. But are we in a position to know the essences of anything?

When we first perceive any material thing, we directly perceive its attributes, but not its essence. The search for the essence of any substance requires that we pay special attention to its formal and final causes. In the case of artefacts, this may seem relatively easy: since we know why cars are made, we can readily grasp why they have the forms they do. When we turn to even the simplest natural things, however, identifying the formal cause becomes incomparably more difficult. Like Aristotle, Aquinas believed that natural things have final causes – goals towards which they naturally strive. As intriguing a notion as this is, it strains credulity for some today, since modern science long ago abandoned final causes as explanatory of natural objects. There is, however, no short-cut to knowledge of the essences of things for Aquinas, since our minds lack the power to penetrate objects except by the painstaking method we have described: carefully distinguishing a thing's essential features from its accidental ones. In a much cited passage, Aquinas dashes our hopes for perfectly knowing essences when he says that 'our cognition is so weak that no philosopher was ever able to investigate perfectly the nature of a single fly: hence it is said that one philosopher spent thirty years in solitude in order to know the nature of a bee.'[22]

Now that we have considered the incompleteness of our knowledge, let us consider the second problem noted above: the fallibility of our intellects. Our intellects are subject to error, but they are not fallible in every respect. Cognitive powers from the senses to the intellect, Aquinas thinks, have a 'proper object' about which they cannot be deceived. The appeal to the proper object serves as a kind of fail-safe for Aquinas's epistemology against skepticism. For if sight failed to detect colour, how else would we would ever discover it? Or if sight could be deceived about colour, how could we possibly correct that error? Despite the importance of this point, Aquinas does not argue for it, but seems to regard it as a self-evident principle.[23]

Likewise, since the intellect has the nature or 'quiddity' of material things as its proper object, it will not fall into error about such natures. This obviously does not mean that we will know natures perfectly, but that our intellect will not *mis*apprehend a nature in such a way as to generate error in all our subsequent thinking about it. Our vulnerability to error increases the further away from the proper object we go. In the case of the senses, their dependence on sense organs means that they can either fail to perceive or mis-perceive the proper object. The colour-blind person simply cannot see certain colours and so fails to apprehend them. The person wearing tinted glasses sees colours darkened by the glass before reaching his eye. Error occurs, however, only when one makes false judgements based on appearances. If I see table salt but do not taste it, I may mistakenly think it is sugar because both are white and come in crystal form. This mistake can be easily corrected by tasting the substance; an error about an 'accidental sensible' (in this case, saltiness) is corrected by the proper sense – in this case, taste. Likewise, an artificially darkened perception of the world can be corrected by removing the tinted glasses. But because the sense powers act through specific organs, a damaged sense organ will fail to perceive its proper object accurately unless and until the organ is restored to normal.

The intellect, by contrast, cannot be affected by a defective organ, since for Aquinas – as we saw in Chapter 3 – it is not the power of any organ. The clearest case for such infallible apprehension concerns indivisible things like circles and squares. Since these can be defined without composition, and composition and division are pre-conditions for falsehood, they are either grasped correctly or not at all.[24] With regard to composite things, however, there are various possibilities for error. Composite definitions can, for instance, contain incompatible terms, or one definition can be falsely predicated of another. Aquinas offers examples that are patently false – a rational animal with wings, a triangular circle – but examples worthy of philosophical reflection could easily be cited. Can a rational animal really be immortal, or is immortality incompatible with animality? Is the definition of a human being as 'rational animal' predicable of any non-human animal that exhibits rationality? Needless to say, most cases drawn from the real world involve composition and so carry with them the risk of error.

As Aquinas sees it, though, neither the limited power of the human intellect nor its fallibility poses insuperable problems for our knowledge.

While human cognition lacks the ability to intuit the essences of things, our capacity to reason makes the natures of material things accessible to knowledge, even if we will never understand them completely. Moreover, our liability to error does not affect the senses or intellect in their first contacts with the objects to which they are specially related. As a result, though we will often be in doubt and sometimes in error, the remedies for these conditions will be those familiar to the empiricist. More experience, and more careful reflection on our experience, will bring most of our epistemic problems under control.

SPIRITUAL COGNITION

We have focused thus far on our cognition of material things, since Aquinas is committed to the idea that these are objects best suited to human knowledge, even if such knowledge in the strict sense of *scientia* is elusive. But where does that leave non-material, or spiritual, objects like the soul, angels and God? Has Aquinas built an epistemology that accounts adequately for our relation to matter, but excludes God? These questions arise because Aquinas has endorsed Aristotle's dictum that human knowing requires a phantasm derived from the material things we sense. Yet there can hardly be phantasms of beings that exist separately from matter. So how are immaterial things to be known?

When we examined his treatment of the soul as form in Chapter 3, we observed that Aquinas believes that he can have the best of Plato's account (subsistence of the soul) and Aristotle's (unity of the person) in a single theory, without the less desirable consequences (mind-body dualism in Plato's case, mortality of the soul in Aristotle's). When he turns to spiritual cognition, he is under no such impression. Non-material objects are either the first things we know, as Plato thought, or the last, as Aristotle did, but they cannot be both. One might think Plato's perspective would seem more attractive to a theologian, but Aquinas's commitment to material things as most proper to our cognitive makeup means that he will align with Aristotle. In addition to the theoretical fit with Aristotle, Aquinas also suggests that our experience supports Aristotle's approach: we pursue knowledge of immaterial beings through material things.[25]

Approaching a more perfect, or 'higher', kind of being from the starting point of a less perfect, or 'lower', being brings with it the limitation that no perfect knowledge of the higher being will be attainable in this way.[26] As Aquinas thinks of it, perfection of being is marked by freedom from material limitations – the less material a substance is, the more perfect it will be. Accordingly, there is a hierarchy of being that places immaterial substances above material ones, angels above human beings, and God above angels. With its superior position to material natures, the human intellect is capable of cognizing the forms of all material things. As we have seen, however, Aquinas's confidence about our intellectual capacity to understand these lower beings is counter-balanced by his sober estimation of how difficult it is to know them completely. In the strictest sense, he thinks that the 'essential principles of things are concealed (*ignota*) from us.'[27] In the case of the mind's self-knowledge, it 'perceives' (*percipit*) itself through its own activity of understanding, yet it must nevertheless seek to know its nature by considering its own acts.[28] Even when we seek to understand our own souls, which are most familiar to us, the method for gaining *scientia* is the same as in the case of knowing material things.

How, then, is human cognition supposed to make the leap from material things to substances entirely separate from matter? For Aquinas, cognition depends on the 'adequation' (*adequatio*) of the mind and the thing, yet a lower type of being can hardly be adequate to a higher type. For a human being to think about immaterial substances like angels is not unlike a dog 'thinking' about a human being. Dogs, at least, are acquainted with human beings; by contrast, the philosopher contemplating angels must rely on likenesses drawn from material things, which would seem to be totally unlike angels, which are immaterial and intelligent.[29] Yet while dogs and angels have no natural genus in common, they both fall into the same *logical* genus of substance. As slim as this basis may seem, it will allow us to reach some positive conclusions about angels based on the common notion of substance.[30] More than that, Aquinas thinks of angels as intelligences without bodies, rather like the human soul when it is separated temporarily from its body after death. While Aquinas is wary of associating the separated soul too closely with angels,[31] he frequently draws comparisons between the human mind and the angelic mind. Like their human analogue, angels also know by means of intelligible species, but in their case the species are innate in their intellects rather than acquired through perception and abstraction, as in our case.

No appeal to a common genus, however, will provide the basis in Aquinas's view for any positive knowledge of God. God is not subject to any genus, since membership in a genus requires that one's quiddity be shared; but the divine essence is unique and incommunicable. It follows from this that God cannot be defined in any conventional way, since definitions rely on genus and difference. For instance, in the definition of the human being as a 'rational animal', the genus is *animal*, while *rational* provides the specific difference, stating the attribute by which we humans differ from other members of the genus *animal*. Without a definition, Aquinas notes, it is also impossible in Aristotelian terms to provide a demonstration of the nature or properties of the divine being.[32]

In Chapter 2, however, we saw that there is another type of demonstration, which begins from effects and works back to the cause. Though a weaker type of demonstration than the *propter quid* type that works from cause to effect, a *quia* demonstration definitively proves the existence of the cause from considering its effects. Aquinas's Five Ways set out to establish the existence of God, but they also add to our knowledge of God on five distinct points. The being whose existence has been demonstrated is (1) an unmoved mover (the ultimate final cause for all beings seeking perfection), (2) the first efficient cause of all else that exists, (3) a necessary being, (4) the most perfect being and (5) a supremely intelligent being that directs all other things to their end. Implicit in these formal descriptions are other attributes that Aquinas will argue belong to God: goodness, providence, creator and so on.

The name *creator* is especially germane to the problem of knowing God. Knowledge, after all, depends on some kind of proportion between the knower and the object to be known. On the face of things, there simply is no proportion between us and God. This is not merely a matter of bridging diverse levels of the hierarchy of being from humans to angels to God. As creator, God is not part of the created order at all.[33] Yet Aquinas is able to find in this most exclusive feature of God – his separateness from all he has created – the basis for a proportion: even if God is not related to creatures, creatures are related to God as effects to their cause.[34] Certainly, God exceeds all his effects in creation, yet whatever perfections we find in those effects must also be present in God, pre-existing in their cause. Inasmuch as we have intellects, we can conclude that God also has an intellect, since he is the author of our intellectual power.[35] Relying on the analogy of being, Aquinas can call our power to know by the same name – intellect (*intellectus*) – as that power in God, even though there are no 'powers' in God separate from the divine essence. Starting from all that we know about the human mind, and prescinding from all its limitations and imperfections, Aquinas offers an extensive account of what the divine intellect must be like.

Notwithstanding God's transcendence and separateness from all created things, Aquinas also holds that God can, and sometimes does, act to enable a more perfect knowledge than human reason can achieve if left to itself. Aquinas speaks of these divine interventions under the term 'grace' (*gratia*). Though we may associate grace especially with salvation, Aquinas's concept of grace includes any empowerment freely given by God. When Aquinas considers whether grace can enable us to attain a more perfect knowledge of God than reason, he does not mean that grace will replace reason or interrupt its activity. Rather, he thinks of grace as strengthening or perfecting the cognitive process.

All human cognition requires the two components of a natural intelligible light (the agent intellect) and images (phantasms) formed from sensible things.[36] Since the human intellect alone fails to find God intelligible, God can graciously infuse additional intellectual 'light' to strengthen the mind's limited power and so illuminate what it seeks to understand.[37] Most importantly, this enables the assent of faith to a divine revelation that would not otherwise be credible to any human mind. While less common, God can also form images directly in one's imagination 'so as to express divine things better than those [images] that we receive naturally from sensible things'.[38] Such is the source of prophetic visions as Aquinas conceives of them.

Given the human intellect's dependence on sensory images to think about any object, as well as its motivation to seek out causes until it reaches a first cause, Aquinas concludes that our minds are always seeking to go beyond their natural limits. It is not so surprising, then, that Aquinas suggests that God will need to provide remedies for the natural weakness of the human intellect. Knowing about God by analogy may provide plenty of grist for philosophers to mill, but it does not suffice for a Christian theology, even one as philosophical as Aquinas's. Yet while Aquinas treats faith as a kind of cognition, and even as certainly true in view of its being revealed by God, he does not equate it with *scientia*.[39] The person with faith can be assured that her beliefs about God are true, but she cannot *know* that they are true. Despite all the help that God gives believers while making their way back to God, there is no direct vision of God until the beatific vision, in which one 'sees' the divine essence. Seeing God face to face requires more than an enhanced capacity of the human intellect; it requires God to unite himself to the intellect. In the present life, however, where no one can claim to know *what* God is, even the closest union with God, whether by reason or by faith, is like being united 'to one unknown'.[40]

CHAPTER 5

ETHICS

Unlike many, and perhaps most contemporary moral philosophers, Aquinas believes that there is an objective purpose to human life. In agreement with Aristotle, he argues that human beings are defined primarily by their rationality, and that human fulfilment lies in the correct use of that capacity. Unlike Aristotle, however, Aquinas rejects the notion that the achievement of this goal is limited to the present life. This belief is rooted partly in Aquinas's adherence to the Christian faith, which holds that all human beings, insofar as they are rational and free, are made in the image of God (*imago Dei*) and accordingly inherit a very special destiny.[1] However, Aquinas is equally emphatic that good philosophical reasons can be provided for holding that the realization of human potential includes a supernatural dimension.

HAPPINESS

That human life as a whole has a goal or an ultimate end has its basis in Aquinas's claim that human action as such is purposive. On Aquinas's view, human beings are 'masters' of their actions in a way that irrational creatures are not, since the latter act primarily according to instinct.[2] When a non-human animal apprehends a predator or some other threat to its survival, it automatically flees from the situation or takes other appropriate measures to preserve itself.[3] Human beings are different. Due to their possession of rationality they are not, so Thomas thinks, similarly constrained in their actions. They too have instincts, but the possession of reason allows them to act against such motives, however powerful, and in accordance with goals other than, say, mere survival. Aquinas calls such deliberate action 'human action' because it is what is distinctive of humans, and it flows from their possession of 'free judgment' (*liberum arbitrium*): the power that comprises the intellect in its capacity for setting personal goals, and the will in its capacity for choosing the means to ends that reason sets for it.

The relevant factor that distinguishes humans from animals, and makes their action moral as such, is that the former are able to deliberate or compare various courses of action and to choose from among alternatives based on their moral principles. Suppose, for example, that a soldier finds himself in a dangerous situation. His instinct for self-preservation will undoubtedly provide a powerful motive for him to flee. But suppose that he has also been habituated to believe that it would be cowardly for a soldier to run away in battle. He clearly has two alternatives (to run or to stand his ground) from which to choose. Aquinas thinks that it is the human power of *liberum arbitrium* that provides the soldier with options about which to deliberate, and therefore with freedom of action, which the non-rational animal lacks. Such action, moreover, is distinctively moral in the sense that we can be held accountable for it, which is why soldiers are punished for deserting their posts. Where actions are determined, as is the case with animals, there is no freedom. And where there is no freedom, so Aquinas thinks, there is no moral responsibility. This is why the possession of rationality is so vital to what it means to be a moral agent: if humans lacked the capacity for free judgement then, as Aquinas points out, 'counsels, encouragements, commands, prohibitions, rewards and punishments would be in vain'.[4]

This of course is not to assert that every action that a human being performs issues from reason and will or is otherwise deliberate. Aquinas recognizes that human beings are capable of a broad array of actions that have no particular moral significance. When a man absent-mindedly strokes his beard or an adolescent girl nervously twirls her hair, they clearly perform rather trivial actions. Likewise when a human being grows or digests his food, although such actions are far from trivial, they lack what is *distinctively* human. Aquinas therefore calls them mere 'actions of men'.[5] Our moral actions, by contrast, *are* distinctively human, issuing as they do from the intrinsic principles of reason and will. They are the actions for which one can be called to account or to provide reasons since they involve a certain self-direction. Accordingly, they either order us to our final end, or they do not.

It is important to bear in mind that Aquinas does not limit purposive action to human beings. He explicitly rejects the view that the possession of reason – or even sense knowledge – is a necessary condition for a created being to act with purpose. Indeed, on Aquinas's view, all of creation, from the planets to the lowest species, from intellectual substances to non-intellectual substances, are subject to final causality. To the extent that a being acts in a determinate fashion, then it acts for the goal of actualizing some potential inherent in it. And to the extent that it acts in such a fashion, it clearly acts with purpose. Insofar as all creatures are striving to actualize their potential, they are striving, so Aquinas thinks, to participate in the perfection of the divine being. The acorn, for instance, always inclines in such a way as to actualize its potential to become an oak tree according to innate principles directing it to achieve such an end. Likewise with the egg's inclination to hatch. But it is also true that, even though all natural beings act purposively, rational agents do so differently from non-rational actors. The difference is that human beings fulfil their purpose by directing *themselves* to their end by means of their wills or 'rational inclinations', while non-rational beings must do so by means of 'natural inclinations' that, implanted by God, necessitate their drive towards perfection.[6] Needless to say, the very same freedom by which rational agents are capable of achieving a higher order of perfection than irrational animals makes them, at the same time, vulnerable to deviations from such an end in a way that irrational beings are not.

Most modern readers will probably have few qualms about conceding to Aquinas the claim that human beings, at least some of the time, act for ends. To the extent that they engage in rational, deliberate action, they can be said to do things on purpose. But what grounds could we possibly have for supposing that because human action has a purpose, human existence as a whole, let alone all creation, does? To put it in medieval terms, why should we think that there is a 'highest good' (*summum bonum*) to human life, or an overaching end (*finis ultimus*) to which all subsidiary ends are ordered? Modern readers will undoubtedly find grounds to be sceptical of this claim for the simple reason that, since at least the Scientific Revolution in the seventeenth century, scientists have overwhelmingly rejected the idea that the universe, including human beings, can be explained in terms of Aristotelian final causality or objective purpose. Rather, according to the dominant modern view, genuine scientific interpretations ought to be restricted to the domain of mechanistic explanations of the universe given that the cosmos operates, not according to final causes inherent in nature, but according to matter and motion alone.[7] Indeed, many modern readers will probably be more sympathetic to Existentialists such as Jean-Paul Sartre (1905–1980) in thinking that if there does exist some purpose to human life, it is one with which we ourselves furnish it.[8]

It is unlikely that Aquinas would have been persuaded by such reasoning. If there were no final end to human life, then humans would have no ultimate basis for motivation. His argument is grounded on the impossibility of an infinite regress in a series of essentially ordered causes. Thomas had used this argument to good effect in some of his famous arguments for the existence of God, and here too he appeals to Aristotle's argument for the existence of a Prime Mover in order to demonstrate analogously the existence of some end that is desired for itself and nothing further.[9] For just as the existence of God or an uncaused cause is necessary to explain motion or alteration in the world, so the existence of something first or ultimate as an object of human rational desire must be posited to account for human motivation. It is clear that human beings act for ends once they form an intention to do so, and then take the necessary steps to execute those intentions. For Aquinas, this signifies that there must be something first both in the order of intention and in the order of execution, for 'if there were no ultimate end nothing would be desired, nor would any act be terminated, nor would the intention of the agent ever be at rest; and if there were no first means in relation to the end, no one would begin to do anything and deliberation would never end, but go on indefinitely.'[10]

What then *is* our final end? Aquinas's term for it is the Latin *beatitudo*, which has commonly been translated into English as 'happiness'. However, the translation of *beatitudo* as 'happiness' can invite misunderstanding. To the modern reader, happiness usually means something akin to subjective contentment. Understood as such, it is dependent on emotional mood, which obviously can fluctuate. When one has a good day, one commonly thinks of oneself as feeling happy; when one does not, one feels sad. But this is not principally what Aquinas means when he uses the term *beatitudo*. Rather, he has something more enduring in mind, which is rooted in his understanding of human nature and his teleological, or purposive, conception of the cosmos.

To grasp how Aquinas understands human happiness, it is useful to see how he defines it in a formal sense. Time and again, he refers to *beatitudo* as 'a perfect and sufficient good that excludes every evil and fulfils every desire'.[11] He also refers to it as that which actualizes our distinctively human potentialities of intellect and will to their fullest possible extent, for 'all agree in desiring the ultimate end because all desire their own perfection, which is what the final end signifies'.[12] Accordingly, happiness can be thought of as having two components, one objective and the other subjective. The former component signifies the good that perfects the creature as its final end, the latter, the operation by which this good is achieved, along with the satisfaction that accompanies such perfection. That happiness as such has these two components arises because when we talk about the final end, which is co-extensive with happiness, the notion of an end can be thought about in two ways: first, as an object, and second, as the possession of that object. The analogy that Aquinas uses is that of the avaricious person, whose goal is both money and the possession of money.[13]

Now Aquinas's requirement that happiness be a perfect, sufficient good that excludes all evil and fulfils every desire effectively rules out several candidates that many moderns would associate with what it means to lead a fulfiling life. Specifically, it appears to exclude such contingent goods as wealth, honour, fame, power and pleasure. What is Aquinas getting at here? Surely there is great satisfaction to be gained, not to mention happiness to be had, by the acquisition of such objects as wealth or a good reputation or the achievement of power. Such things are undoubtedly goods in direct proportion as their opposites are evils. No rational person would choose a life of grinding poverty for its own sake, or desire to be subjected to the ridicule or exploitation of others. And Aquinas would emphatically agree that the opposites of such evils are fitting objects of rational desire.

He is not suggesting, then, that the good life can only be achieved by adopting the existence of the monkish ascetic who shuns material possessions and eschews all pleasures. Rather, his point is that none of the foregoing can qualify, from a purely logical or definitional standpoint, as the *highest* good. Money or wealth cannot be what happiness ultimately consists in, because happiness is the final end, while riches are simply a means towards the end of sustenance, which in turn is the means towards leading a good life.[14] Likewise, honours are simply an indication that one is happy or virtuous. To confuse honour with happiness is therefore to confuse the sign with the thing signified. No doubt there is, or ought to be, a connection between honour and virtue to the extent that a good reputation frequently follows recognition of a virtuous character. But the two things, so Thomas thinks, should not be confused.[15]

We need not itemize the specific reasons why each of the afore-mentioned goods cannot qualify as the *finis ultimus* for Aquinas.[16] In general, however, his principal reason for excluding any created good from comprising the ultimate end is based on the compelling psychological observation that no temporal good, either alone or taken together, can completely satisfy the human desire for happiness. Aquinas sees human beings, much as St. Augustine did, as restless creatures who are always seeking to achieve some good or satisfy some aspect of their personality. Such a restless and anxious existence can only come to an end once happiness – the 'perfect good that completely brings desire to rest' – is achieved.[17] But there is no good achievable in the present life, or so Thomas thinks, that can bring desire to rest. Even should one become extremely rich, say, one will still desire other goods, whether these be health, honours, loyalty, love or wisdom. This is because, given the psychological structure of human beings, when it comes to temporal goods, 'as soon as such things are possessed, they are despised and other things are desired.'[18] Indeed, according to Aquinas, the possession of these goods pro-vides an even deeper awareness that happiness is to be found elsewhere, because 'we recognize their insufficiency all the more when we possess them, which consequently shows their imperfection and that the ultimate good does not consist in them.'[19] Besides, if happiness is the highest good, then it follows that it must be incom-patible with any evil. Unfortunately, the present life is altogether too vulnerable to setbacks that are impossible to avoid, among which Aquinas lists 'the evil of ignorance on the part of the intellect, the evil of inordinate affection on the part of desire, and the evil of much suffering on the part of the body'.[20]

What object *can* completely satisfy the innate human desire for happiness? This, of course, is God, who is uncreated and the source of all created goods which merely participate in his goodness. He is the Creator and the ultimate source of all things as well as pure act or perfection, without any potentiality.[21]

One of the chief sources of anxiety and frustration in the present life is associated with the fact that we are rational creatures. Accordingly, we are constantly striving to understand the world in as complete a way as possible, but in this life we can never know – in the deepest sense of knowing – the ultimate cause of things, because we only have access to the effects of the Creator. Such knowledge as can be attained in the present life is therefore imperfect, as is the happiness that is associated with it. Accordingly, perfect happiness can only be achieved once our intellects are completely actualized, and this only happens if and when we achieve direct experience of God in the beatific vision. [22] As Aquinas puts it, 'with respect to perfect happiness, the intellect must attain to the very essence of the first cause and then it will have its perfection by union with God as its object.'[23]

Because Aquinas regarded ultimate happiness as consisting in the perfection of the intellect, he distinguished himself from his Franciscan contemporaries who typically claimed that love, which is an act of the will, rather than understanding, is what ultimately unites rational beings to God.[24] Aquinas rejects this claim on the ground that, if happiness is the achievement of the final end, this cannot consist in an act of the will, since the will is an inclination for objects which are not present, and a capacity for enjoying objects once achieved. This is not to say, however, that the will does not play an important role in the achievement of happiness. Rather, it is only to say that it plays an accidental, rather than essential, one.[25]

Aquinas thinks, then, that the natural longing for complete happiness is rooted in the universal desire for God. If the ultimate end accounts for why we are motivated to do anything, and God is our ultimate end, then it seems to follow, according to Aquinas, that God is our main source of motivation in all of our actions. But this is surely an implausible notion for at least two reasons. First, can we really say that we are desiring union with God when we choose, say, to opt for a career in law over a career in medicine? Second, it just seems to be empirically false that all desire God when it is manifestly clear that many people reject the existence of such a being. We must therefore be very clear on what Aquinas has in mind here. And what he means is that, to the extent that in all of our significant choices we are seeking to actualize or perfect some potentiality, then we are seeking to become God-like, even if we are not immediately aware of it.

To conclude: for Aquinas all human beings seek happiness. Whenever they will anything, they do so under the aspect of the good (*sub ratione boni*). That is, they are seeking to perfect themselves or actualize their potential and, knowingly or not, they are trying to get back to God (who is pure actuality). This is true of everything in creation. All beings, rational or non-rational, to the extent that they are in potency and are trying to actualize their potential, are striving to return to God (*plenitudo essendi*). But, of course, rational creatures attain participation in the divine in a different way: we do it by means of reason and will. However, the possession of reason and will also makes it such that we can fail to achieve our final end. If we lead a virtuous life, we will perfect ourselves and, with the assistance of God, experience the beatific vision. If not, we will experience alienation from the source of all being. Other creatures, however, have innate principles that lead them back to God. The result of possessing free decision is that it makes us vulnerable as far as achieving the final end is concerned. For the same principles of reason and will that allow human beings to participate in the divine being in a more 'excellent way' if used correctly, can also be the source of failure to achieve the final end if used incorrectly. Hence, the need for the virtues as internal guides to happiness, and the natural law as an external one.

THE NATURAL LAW

When Aquinas refers to the 'natural law' (*lex naturalis*), he does not have in mind physical principles such as the law of gravity. Rather, he is referring to the existence of a moral law whose principles are timeless and universal. Their purpose is not simply to regulate behaviour between people – although such principles certainly form part of the *lex naturalis* – but, equally importantly, to direct rational agents towards achieving happiness or self-perfection. Because these basic moral principles are the same for all people at all times and places, Thomas clearly thinks that they are independent of human convention and individual desire. Aquinas is therefore a proponent of what we would nowadays call moral realism, part of which theory involves a rejection of such commonly held contemporary views as that moral norms are relative to human culture or an expression of individual attitude or desire, and, hence, subjective. For Aquinas, moral rules can be apprehended by reason and are therefore – in principle, anyway – knowable by all.

The natural law tradition, of which Aquinas is one of the most prominent representatives, is an ancient one. Intimations of it can be found in Greek tragedy, political oratory and philosophy.[26] That it was possible to distinguish between moral norms that are rooted in convention and 'a law valid for all men given by nature', as the great orator and statesman Demosthenes (384–322 BC) put it, was a guiding thread throughout much of ancient Greek culture. One can detect the distinction as early as in the fragments of Heraclitus (*ca.* 540–475 BC), and it is particularly prominent in the disputes between Socrates and the Sophists in several of Plato's dialogues.[27] Indeed it is arguably even present in Aristotle's *Nicomachean Ethics*, where he famously draws a distinction between 'natural justice', or the cluster of rules and principles for action that are valid in all places and do not depend on human will or acceptance, and 'legal justice', or those rules that are established by human convention and can therefore vary from place to place (1134b18–1135a14). As far as pagan influences on the Christian tradition are concerned, however, it was Stoicism that provided the most coherent and sustained account of natural law, passing into Latin political and moral culture mainly by way of Cicero (106–43 BC), who exerted considerable influence on medieval moral thinking by pointing to a 'true law' that is associated with 'right reason, consistent with nature, known to all, unchanging, eternal, which calls to duty by its prescriptions [and] deters from wrong by its prohibitions'.[28] From here, it was only a short step for St. Paul to invoke, in however inchoate a way, a universal law that 'is written in the hearts of men' (Rom. 2:15).[29] Next to Cicero, perhaps no Roman author had more influence on Aquinas's thinking with respect to law than that of the jurist Ulpian (d. 228).[30]

Before we turn to Aquinas's understanding of the natural law we need to see how he understands law as such, since the natural law is only one species of law, along with the eternal law, human law and the divine law. To see why something counts as a law, then, as opposed to some other sort of rule or command, we need to understand how Thomas understands the essence of law. Otherwise, we will fail to properly appreciate the metaphysical assumptions that underpin his account.

At its most general, law is 'nothing else than an ordinance of reason for the common good, made by someone who has care of the community, and promulgated'.[31] If we parse this definition carefully, we will notice that law, for Thomas, has four features. First of all, it is a command of reason. By stating this, Aquinas is explicitly rejecting what is sometimes called 'theological voluntarism', the medieval school of thought that claimed that the norms of law and morality are ultimately rooted in the will of God. Against this view, Thomas argues that law is something pertaining to reason. It is not, of course, because he denies the existence of God that he is reluctant to ground law and morality in the divine will. Rather, it is that to link such commands to any will, divine or human, is ultimately to disconnect it from reason. It is to make, in short, moral norms entirely arbitrary. Finally, to reduce morality ultimately to the divine will leaves human beings altogether too reliant on scripture and revelation for knowledge of its principles. Aquinas wants to ensure that *all* human beings, by virtue of their natures, have access to the universal norms of morality which, he thinks, hold at all times and places.

How then is law related to reason? Briefly put, law and reason are related because both perform the identical function of providing a rule and a measure of actions. Law provides a rule in that it guides human beings in their actions, directing them to do things that will help them to actualize their potential and contribute to the common good. It provides a measure, obviously, in that if something fails or refrains from being so directed, then they do something that violates the law. But, for Thomas, practical reason *also* provides a rule and a measure of human actions. It too directs rational agents in that it is practical reason that furnishes ends and then sets about finding the most effective means of achieving those ends. Reason therefore rules human actions in the sense that it guides them in ways that will help them to achieve our goals. To the extent that our choices contribute to our final end, then, they are rational; to the extent that they do not, they are irrational.[32] Rationality therefore provides a measure, much as law does, for our actions.

The second condition for a rule or principle to be considered a genuine law is that it must by definition serve the common good. This is because, as we have seen, law is related to practical reason, the most basic object of which is the good. Ultimately, of course, this is God, who is the final end of all creatures to the extent that they are striving to actualize their potential. Law therefore must contribute to the happiness or perfection of all of the beings that fall under its guidance. It is of the definition of law, then, that it serves the universal happiness or common good.[33] As far as this principle applies to human beings, it entails that any law that does not contribute to the flourishing of all of the members of the community cannot by definition be considered a valid law. Rather, for Thomas, it is a perversion of law. On this account, any rule that seeks only to benefit a certain class of people, like laws that segregate the races for the benefit of whites, say, would not be legitimate on Aquinas's view. Rather, law must contribute to the flourishing of *all* members of the community by directing them to lead virtuous lives. As Thomas puts it, 'since virtue makes its possessors good, the proper effect of law is to make its subjects good, either without qualification or in some respect.'[34]

Third, the ability to make laws belongs either to the entire populace or to a person who has care of the community. Whether the legislator of the community turns out to be a group of people or a single person does not seem to bother Aquinas, so long as they rule in the interests of the community and disseminate laws that serve the common good.[35] However, a key feature of the legitimacy of the lawmaker is that they cannot be private citizens. Rather, they must hold public office since they require the power of coercion – that is, command over the police and the military – to be at their disposal. Why should this be the case? So that the law may be effective.[36] The implication here is that, although human beings are rational animals who are naturally inclined to seek the good, they are nonetheless also inclined to make choices that frustrate the proper achievement of this goal. This claim undoubtedly arises from Aquinas's adherence to the doctrine of original sin. For Aquinas, human beings are not perfect, nor are they perfectible. Rather, they possess a powerful and innate drive to make selfish, anti-social choices that thwart their relationships with other human beings as well as God. Hence, the need for social institutions – not to mention divine assistance – to keep such drives in check, and public offices that are vested with the legitimate power to punish those who disobey the law.

A final condition is that laws must be widely disseminated or promulgated if they are to impose obligations on individuals.[37] As a natural-law thinker, Aquinas holds the view that law and morality are connected, indeed that there is a conceptual, logical connection between the two. As he famously puts it, a law that is not morally just, is not a law. Rather, it is a perversion of law. Indeed, such commands are more like acts of 'violence' than anything else.[38] Such a rule cannot therefore, so Thomas thinks, generate obligations. Since it is the case that any law must by definition give rise to an obligation, the non-observance of which one can be punished for, justice seems to demand that those who fall under the law be notified of its contents. Obviously this rules out secret or retroactive laws from being just and therefore genuine.[39]

As far as the different kinds of laws are concerned, the most foundational is the eternal law (*lex aeterna*). All of the other laws – natural, human and divine – are simply derivations of it. In its most basic sense, the eternal law comprises those principles that reflect God's rational governance of the entire universe. Because God is all powerful and all knowing, he has created a providential universe. He orders all things, rational and irrational, animate and inanimate, to their ends. In the case of irrational beings, he does so by implanting natural drives and inclinations that permit them to achieve their full potential. Insofar as they achieve the actualization of their potential, they reflect the perfection of the Creator. That fire is inclined to rise and to heat its surroundings, for instance, or that the acorn is inclined to grow into an oak tree, is evidence of a law that directs everything in the universe in a deliberate fashion.[40] The eternal law, in short, is confirmation of Aquinas's belief that the universe is not a random, meaningless place. Rather, it is inherently rational and purposive since it is governed by an omniscient God.

Unlike irrational beings, rational creatures are capable of guiding themselves to their end. In this respect, they are like God.[41] Unfortunately, the capacity for self-direction and independent action that makes rational agents more godlike than other creatures also comes with the risk that they will fall short of their final end. Non-rational beings may share in the divine perfection in a diminished way compared to rational beings, but they are not similarly vulnerable. They deterministically act for their own good since they are directed by means of inclinations which are hardwired, as it were, into their very natures. Humans are also hardwired to seek happiness. They too have a natural tendency, so Thomas thinks, to perform actions that they think will actualize their specifically human potential.[42] However, they also possess freedom of choice (*liberum arbitrium*), which permits them a plurality of valid ways to achieve happiness. It also means that they are invariably vulnerable to making choices that will ultimately frustrate their ability to achieve the ultimate end. The natural law exists, then, as a guide to help rational agents achieve happiness. It is, as Thomas puts it, an 'imprint of the divine light' on the rational being, which consists essentially in those principles and precepts that, if properly grasped and followed, will lead rational agents to self-perfection.[43] The natural law is simply, so Thomas thinks, the eternal law as inscribed in the human heart.

How do humans come to know the moral precepts that comprise the natural law? Although Aquinas is an empiricist who therefore rejects the belief that humans have innate knowledge of anything, he nonetheless accepts the view that rational beings possess certain natural *dispositions* towards acquiring knowledge. And just as the intellect has a natural disposition to apprehend the most basic truths in the realm of speculative reason, so too it has a certain natural disposition or inclination to apprehend those principles that form the basis of the natural law. Aquinas calls this the inborn habit of *synderesis*, and it is the special disposition that human beings possess which allows them to apprehend the most basic principles in the realm of practical reason.[44]

According to Aquinas, then, all knowledge must ultimately be grounded in certain self-evident truths. In the realm of speculative reason, which provides rational beings with knowledge of matters that cannot be otherwise, the most basic axiom of all thinking is the principle of non-contradiction. Sometimes called a classic law of thought, this principle states that the same thing cannot be affirmed and denied at the same time, since to do so would be to contradict oneself, which is irrational.[45] It is understood to be a fundamental law of thought when it comes to our understanding of the world because it is based on the most basic *concepts* of thought: namely, *being* and *not-being*. Whenever we come to know something about the world, we develop an understanding of it as a specific sort of being. All speculative knowledge, then, is based on the notion that, to the extent that something exists, it does not merely have being, but has a certain *type* of being.

In the realm of practical reason, which is directed towards knowledge for the sake of action, by contrast, the most basic concept is not being, but *good*. By this Aquinas means that whenever rational beings make choices, they do so because they think that they will result in the achievement of a good that will fulfil them in some way. He believes, in short, that being a rational agent involves, at least in part, the notion that one always makes choices under the aspect of the good. We might be mistaken about what our genuine good is at any given time, of course, but this does not prevent us from making the assumption that the objects we are pursuing are somehow *good* when we undertake deliberate, and therefore uniquely human, actions.[46]

According to Aquinas, then, just as the first principle of speculative reason is founded on the notion of 'being', so the first principle of practical reason is founded on the notion of 'good'. Accordingly, the first principle of practical reason is 'good is that which all things seek after.' For Aquinas, this amounts to a self-evident proposition, similar to propositions such as 'All bachelors are male,' or 'Every man is mortal.' How so? Because a self-evident proposition is one in which the predicate term is included in the meaning of the subject term. Just as *maleness* is included in the definition of 'bachelor' and *mortality* in the definition of 'man', so the notion of *being desirable* or *sought after* is included in the very definition of 'goodness'.

This self-evident principle of practical reason generates a command or a precept stating that 'good is to be done and pursued and evil avoided' (*bonum est faciendum et prosequendum, et malum vitandum*). Other precepts will correctly follow insofar as they are consistent with this basic precept, that is, insofar as they actually contribute to the final good of human beings, which is happiness, or to the common good. Now, a potential problem with the first fundamental precept is that it appears to be empty of content. It urges us to pursue the good, but it does not seem to be very explicit about how to *define* the good. Some people regard pleasure as the good, for example, while other people identify ultimate value with money or power. Is the good, then, simply relative to one's attitudes and preferences? The answer, of course, is no. How then do we fill in the content of the term 'good'? We look to our natural inclinations. If we are naturally disposed towards certain objects, then this must mean, so Thomas thinks, that they are good and therefore worth achieving. As he puts it: 'since good has the nature of an end, and evil, the nature of its contrary, accordingly, all those things to which man has a natural inclination are naturally apprehended by reason as being good, and therefore as objects of pursuit, and their contraries as evil, and therefore objects of avoidance.'[47] Put otherwise, when rational beings have a natural inclination towards something, this fact generates a corresponding moral precept obligating them to pursue it.

Aquinas's classic treatment of the natural law in *Summa theolo-giae*, I-II, q. 94, a. 2 identifies three general types of inclinations that give rise to corresponding precepts. The most basic inclination that follows from the injunction to pursue good and avoid evil is one that rational beings share with all living beings, namely the tendency towards self-preservation. For Aquinas, such an inclination gives rise to a moral dictate that rational agents take the appropriate steps necessary to keep themselves in existence, and to avoid the evil of annihilation and death.[48] This will presumably mean pursuing such objects as an adequate supply of food and drink, and the avoidance of such evils as hunger, self-imposed starvation and suicide. The second inclination that Aquinas identifies is one that human beings share with animals, namely, their tendency to engage in sexual intercourse with a view to procreation. This inclination generates a moral injunction urging rational beings to contribute to the continuation of the species and to look after their offspring.[49] Finally, humans have a species-specific inclination towards the good as apprehended by reason. This is clear from the fact that we have wills (*voluntates*), or rational tendencies, towards self-perfection. But since we only achieve such perfection by living in society, by worship-ping God and leading good, properly *human* lives, this inclination to the good in general will give rise to obligations enjoining us to avoid anti-social acts – such as theft, murder and so on – that ultimately undermine the foundations of society. It will also enjoin us to pursue the moral and intellectual virtues, and to practise religion.[50]

In pointing to inclinations that all human beings share as a basis for our knowledge of ethical principles, Aquinas believes that he is outlining a theory of morality that is applicable to all people, at all times, and in all places. He is advocating, in other words, a universal morality that all should recognize. But how can Aquinas claim that moral norms are the same for all people? Is it not manifestly clear that human practices differ, and should we not therefore conclude from this that morals, far from being universally agreed upon, are in fact completely relative to individuals and cultures? After all, some cultures think it a requirement of morality that females be circum-cised when they reach a certain age, while other cultures regard that practice as an abomination. Likewise, some individuals in our culture regard homosexual behaviour as morally illicit, while others do not. Does this not show that moral practices, and therefore the norms on which they are grounded, are simply contingent matters? Aquinas is quite aware of these objections and has an answer to them.

There are several reasons, so Thomas thinks, why customs and morals may vary over time or across cultures. First, human beings are fallible. They are prone to intellectual error and bad habits which, taken together or separately, often cause ignorance of what the natural moral law truly prescribes. Take the practice and institution of slavery. For centuries it was thought entirely normal in almost every civilization and culture that has existed for some people to enslave others for their own benefit. Although slavery still exists in some parts of the modern world, most if not all enlightened people today regard such a practice as barbaric. Does this not decisively demonstrate that morality is contingent? Our ancestors approved of it, but we do not. How can we possibly say that they were wrong and we are right? They did not *think* that they were doing anything particularly wrong in enslaving others, presumably; otherwise they would not have approved of the practice nor engaged in it.

This is a common gambit for the relativist or emotivist to play. But the natural law proponent has a response to this objection. People in the past may have thought that slavery was morally acceptable, the natural law theorist will admit, but they were *wrong*. How could they make such an error? A plausible explanation is that they based the practice on mistaken assumptions, which became entrenched over time, about the people they were enslaving. They likely thought of them as less rational and therefore less human, and accordingly not deserving of the same treatment as they afforded themselves. Aristotle, for example, famously justified slavery along these lines.[51] We now know, however, that those who defended slavery in the past suffered from a certain ignorance about the facts. Advances in our scientific knowledge about human beings demonstrates, in ways that were perhaps unavailable to our ancestors, that there is no essential or generic difference between the souls of some human beings and the souls of others that justifies one group treating the other as inferior, as Aristotle believed. Moral norms, in other words, have not changed, according to the proponent of natural law. What has changed is that we now have a more accurate assessment about the nature of human beings, and thus a more accurate idea of how to apply the general principles of the natural law as they pertain to treating others. The example of slavery, then, is an example of how a vicious custom that has built up over time can blind people to the true nature of the objective moral law.[52]

Second, bad moral habits, such as become ingrained in vicious people, or the influence of strong passions, as happens in people who suffer from moral weakness, can also blind individuals to what the natural law truly enjoins. Human beings are subject to the burden of original sin, after all, which makes it a continual struggle for them to do what is right. Applying the moral law to specific circumstances can be particularly difficult, then, in people who have developed strong emotions, which can often cloud their judgement as to how to apply the principles of the moral law.[53]

Third – and this is why human law (*lex humana*) is necessary – laws may vary from time to time or place to place not because there is anything like essential disagreement between communities, but because there are sometimes any number of ways in which the most basic precepts of natural law can be realized. This is because the more specific the derivations or determinations from general principles become, the more room there is for variation. Take the notion of justice as a general principle. All reasonable people agree on the fundamental assumption that for any society to function, those of its members who commit acts that threaten the common good must be punished. This is a simple matter of justice, and thus a basic precept of the natural law. Accordingly, all societies will rightly have the following provision built into their moral and legal codes: 'If you do something wrong, you will be punished.' However, societies may sometimes differ, for historical or cultural reasons, perhaps, on how to apply the law with respect to punishment. Hence, no society can properly function if people are not punished, to provide an obvious example, for committing murder. But whether a murderer receives the death penalty or a life sentence is going to depend, not just on right reason arriving at correct conclusions about how to apply general principles of justice, but also on historical and cultural factors. The punishment may differ in its specific application, so Thomas thinks, but the moral fact that murder is an illicit act that must be punished remains consistent across communities.[54]

Human laws, then, may differ from place to place or time to time, but such variations will often be merely superficial. A culture in which one man may have many wives, for example, serves the natural inclination towards sexual activity with a view to procreation in the same way that monogamy does. Sexual relations with members of a different species, by contrast, do not serve this purpose, and are therefore illicit from the perspective of the natural law. Such practices, in short, help to explain why cultures may *appear* to differ with respect to their moral codes, but where, so long as their applications are consistent with the natural law, they will be perfectly licit.

The final type of law that Aquinas recognizes is the divine law (*lex divina*), which comprises those precepts that are revealed in scripture. Why should humans need a law above and beyond the natural law to guide them in their actions? There are several reasons, Thomas thinks, why the divine law is necessary. For one thing, the natural law merely provides prescriptions for leading a good life in the here and now. But recall, above and beyond natural, earthly happiness human beings are also ordered to a supernatural destiny that consists in union with the Creator through the beatific vision. Because this goal exceeds human natural capacities it is necessary, so Thomas thinks, that man have a higher law that directs him to such an end.[55] That God should provide a divine law is also useful since – as we have seen – it is often no easy matter to apply the natural law in specific circumstances.[56] The Decalogue, then, provides straightforward commands that all people can follow.

In sum, Aquinas's theory of natural law provides rational beings with an objective set of moral prescriptions that can be apprehend naturalistically. To act morally, as we have seen, means to act in accordance with our natures. Since human nature is essentially associated with rationality, this will obviously mean that we ought to act in a rational way, which for Thomas means to act in ways that are conducive to achieving happiness. According to this view, if our deliberate actions contribute to happiness or self-perfection, then they are consistent with right reason and, hence, the natural law. If not, then they are irrational, illicit and contrary to nature.

A potential problem for Aquinas arises from his claim that the content of the good can be derived from an examination of human natural inclinations. The natural law, as we saw in the foregoing discussion, claims that human beings have moral obligations to act in ways that do not undermine the common good. This prescription is in turn is based on the fact that human beings have an inclination to live in society, since only in large groups can they achieve anything approaching self-perfection. At the same time, however, humans also appear have an evident, and perfectly *natural*, inclination towards committing selfish, anti-social acts. However, if both are equally natural, we might reasonably wonder why the former inclination should be used to fill in the content of the good and not the latter? Likewise, human beings, on the whole, have inclinations to towards uniting sexually with others, including with members of the same gender. Why, then, should the only licit expression of such an inclination come exclusively in the form of the heterosexual institution of marriage?

Once again, the answer to the foregoing questions is going to involve the fact that such inclinations must, for Aquinas, be shaped in *rational* ways. Human beings do indeed have a natural inclination towards engaging in intercourse with others. But such inclinations must be shaped, so Thomas thinks, in reasonable ways if they are to lead to happiness rather than misery. This will mean that sexual intercourse, according to the natural law, should be pursued only in certain circumstances, with certain people, and for the right reasons. Such constraints will rule out – because they are disordered and contrary to nature – such practices as engaging in sexual relations with members of the same sex or of a different species, with all and sundry, and so on. Likewise each rational being has an inclination to keep himself in being, part of which obviously entails taking appropriate steps to feed ourselves. But, like the inclination towards sex, we must satisfy the inclination towards taking nourishment in a rational way, which will obviously rule out such practices as gluttonous behaviour, or eating as much as possible for the sheer pleasure of it, as disordered. And so on.

It is perhaps at this point becoming a little clearer that a certain type of wisdom is necessary for leading the moral life. For we need to use our reason, not to *rationalize* our behaviour and selfish desires, as some philosophers think, but to *discover* the various and myriad ways in which it is possible to achieve full human potential. The natural law provides us with sound albeit general principles. Unfortunately, the moral life consists not just in knowing abstract principles, but in their application to concrete, individual actions that can be realized in many different ways. Put otherwise, because there are many options open to us as free individuals, we will need a certain amount of prudence, or practical wisdom (*prudentia*), in order to live well. This is where the moral virtues, for Aquinas, become relevant. For Aquinas, right reason must always be the measure of our actions. We cannot go wrong if we act in accordance with our natures – our natural inclinations – so long as we do this in a rational way. What is the measure of acting in such a way? For Aquinas, it means acting virtuously.[57] Natural law and virtue, then, are closely tied.

THE VIRTUES

Aquinas is emphatic in his belief that leading a good, self-fulfiling life consists not merely in doing the right thing, but in having a good character. This places him in a tradition that goes back to the ancient Greeks, for whom the central question of moral philosophy is not simply, as tends to be the case with much modern philosophy, 'What is the right thing to do?' Rather, the central question for Aquinas and his Greek predecessors is also and perhaps even more importantly, 'What sort of person is it good to be?' Aquinas is often thought of as a natural-law thinker, which of course he is. Yet he is also very much a part of the Western tradition of what is now called virtue ethics. This is because his views on the importance of admirable character traits to a life well lived very much complement his views on the importance of following the prescriptions of the natural law.

In the previous section we saw that the natural law provides us with an account of the various ends of human life. At the same time, the goals that it prescribes are very general and, as it were, abstract. This can generate a certain disconnect, as it were, between the principles that are supposed to order the moral life, and the moral life itself, which is comprised of individual human actions. Put otherwise, to live a concrete, specifically good human life involves not just *knowing* what it is right to do in the myriad situations that comprise a proper human life, but in the acquisition of dispositions (*habitus*) that will make it easier for us to put our moral knowledge into practice. These are called virtues.[58] For Thomas, then, the natural law directs rational agents to their ultimate end from without, as it were, by providing objective moral principles, while the virtues direct them to such an end from within.

Although Aquinas emphasizes the centrality of reason in his account of the moral life, this should not lead us to think that he denigrates the importance of the emotions and the appetites, the possession of which are part and parcel of what it means to be human.[59] For although we are primarily defined by our rationality, we also have desires, both visceral and intellectual, which influence the moral life in all sorts of complex ways. Such inclinations contribute to the ultimate end if shaped properly and detract from it, if not.

We should not suppose, however, that disorders on the part of the lower desires – as when some people place sex, food and wine as their highest objects of pursuit – are the only type of disorders that derail us from leading a life worthy of a human being. The moral life is complex because the human animal is complex. This is why the virtues are important. For unlike animals, with whom human beings share the capacity for feeling and desiring individual things, human beings also possess reason and will. Unfortunately, these faculties can also go wrong either through error, which is a disorder in the intellect, or malice, which is a disorder in the will. Accordingly, they can thwart our abilities to achieve the true good as much as any disorder in the sense appetites. Hence, the need for the virtues: habits of the soul that perfect the will, the intellect and sensory appetites, ordering these faculties in such a way as to assist the agent who possesses them to achieve happiness.

In some respects, Aquinas's theory of the virtues is deeply influenced by Aristotle, as when Aquinas often defines a virtue as 'the fulfilment of a capacity'.[60] In other important ways, however, his attitude to the virtues is radically different. In the *Summa theologiae* and the *Disputed Questions on the Virtues in General*, for example, Aquinas endorses the definition of virtue that the twelfth-century theologian Peter Lombard (*ca.* 1100–1160) had attributed to Augustine.[61] According to that definition, 'virtue is a good quality of the mind by which we live rightly, which no one misuses, and which God works in us without our help.'[62] Clearly this is a much more theological understanding of virtue than Aristotle would have endorsed. This is because, in addition to the naturally acquired intellectual and moral virtues that Aristotle counted as constitutive of his naturalistic account of happiness, Aquinas adds a set of theological virtues that are supposed to direct rational beings to the perfect happiness of the beatific vision.[63] Because the direct vision of God is a supernatural end, it requires, so Thomas thinks, supernaturally infused virtues for its achievement. St. Thomas also allows for the possibility that, in some cases, God directly infuses the virtues into certain people.[64] Aristotle, by contrast, would not have recognized faith, hope and charity as virtues, still less would he have thought that God bestows the moral virtues on some individuals without any action on their part.

Rather, Aristotle preferred to think that such qualities are acquired by natural means.[65]

Because the virtues are qualities of the soul that assist rational beings in living rightly, according to Aquinas, it follows that the intellectual virtues – understanding, wisdom, and so on – are only virtues in a qualified sense.[66] Aristotle would undoubtedly have disagreed with this, because he valued the life of philosophical contemplation, along with the life of moral and political activity, as a valid – and arguably superior – way to achieve human happiness.[67] For Aristotle, then, the intellectual virtues, particularly the virtue of theoretical contemplation (*theōria*), were therefore considered virtues in the fullest sense of the term. This is not to argue that Aristotle completely separated intellectual virtue from moral virtue, only that he saw the intellectual virtues as equally worthy of the name of virtue. However, if one defines virtue, as Aquinas does, as a quality that makes its possessor 'good', then it is easy to see how virtue can become more or less exclusively associated with morality.[68]

For Aquinas, then, virtues are qualities of the soul that are by definition incapable of being abused, nor are they compatible with evil. These requirements are not necessarily true of the intellectual virtues. Indeed it is very easy to conceive of someone who excels at mathematics or logic, but who is nonetheless sexually promiscuous or unfair to others. Some of the intellectual virtues can, moreover, be abused. One can easily imagine a great scientist who, though brilliant in his field and possessed of a superior knowledge of the natural world, is nonetheless entirely unscrupulous and willing to put his talents to nefarious ends in exchange for money. Such a person possesses the 'virtue' of science, that is, superior knowledge of the way the world is, but is clearly not a virtuous *person*. Aquinas's basic intuition, then, is that to count as a virtuous person one must first and foremost to be a *morally* good person. Aquinas arguably shares this intuition with us today.

The one intellectual virtue that is inextricably linked to the moral virtues, and without which it is impossible to lead a good human life, is the excellence of mind known as prudence or practical wisdom (*prudentia*). For contemporary English speakers, the term *prudence* will invariably carry connotations associated with possessing a cautious temperament or with being thrifty. However, this is not primarily what Aquinas had in mind. Indeed we achieve a much better idea of what he meant by the term *prudentia* once we realize that it is a contraction of the Latin word *providentia*, which literally means 'foresight', and is obviously the source of our word 'providence'. As Aquinas puts it, quoting Isidore of Seville (*ca.* 560–636), 'a prudent man is one who sees as it were from afar, for his sight is keen, and he foresees the uncertain events.'[69] Prudence is therefore, so Thomas thinks, habitually demonstrating foresight or good judgement when it comes to making practical decisions; or, as he puts it, it is 'right reason of things to be done'.[70] It is, in short, the ability to know what choices to make in which situations in order to attain happiness, and it is absolutely vital to the moral life.

In addition to practical wisdom, Aquinas lists courage (*fortitudo*), temperance (*temperantia*) and justice (*iustitia*) as the virtues on which the moral life turns. These four dispositions – one intellectual and three moral – he calls the 'cardinal virtues', so-called from the Latin word *cardo*, meaning, 'hinge'. We have seen why practical wisdom is crucial to leading a good human life. But what is the rationale for giving such pride of place to the others? Why should we count temperance and courage as the moral dispositions on which the good life hinges and not, say, charm, wit or generosity? We saw above that our desires, more than any other part of the soul, can contribute to our happiness or detract from it. A person who is perpetually angry at the world or one who is excessively anxious, even when there is little reason to be, is generally an unhappy person. It is therefore important that our desires be brought into line with our principles. There is much room in the good life for satisfying one's appetites, on Thomas's account, but this must be done in a rational way. The moral virtues, therefore, correspond to the appetitive or desiring parts of the soul.

The moral virtues, then, are the appetites or inclinations of the soul insofar as they have been shaped in ways that make them responsive to right reason. Justice disposes the agent who possesses such a virtue to give to others their due.[71] It is located in and perfective of the will – the rational appetite that inclines agents towards the good – since respecting what is owed to others is a fundamental constituent of human happiness. Courage perfects, and is located in the irascible part of the sensory appetite, moderating such emotions as fear and anger.[72] Finally, temperance perfects what Aquinas calls the concupiscible part of the sense appetite, disposing its subject to place rational limits on the inclination towards visceral pleasure.[73] All other virtues can be subsumed under the foregoing.

Now it is Aquinas's view that once one has prudence, then one will have all of the other cardinal virtues, and vice versa. In other words – and Aquinas shares this doctrine with such thinkers as Aristotle and Plato before him – the virtues are all connected in such a way that if you have one, then you must have them all. This seems like an implausible claim. Why should we suppose that if a soldier is brave on the battlefield he will necessarily be temperate with respect to, say, sex? But Aquinas's conceptual commitments make the unity of the virtues necessary. If practical wisdom involves making sound practical judgements, and these in turn involve having a correct assessment of which ends are appropriate to rational beings, then it seems to follow that if one possesses the virtue of prudence, then this must be because one's appetitive powers are in harmony with their rational principles.[74] This is because the manner in which the end appears to an agent very much depends on what sort of character he has. If a person has been habituated in such a way that they cannot resist the prompting of their libido, and moreover are quite comfortable with the idea of being sexually promiscuous, then this will naturally influence the sort of choices they make. They will regard as good any opportunity for sex, and end up sleeping with all and sundry. If, however, the virtues have been instilled in the appetitive powers, one will naturally have a more correct assessment of the final end, which will then determine what choices one ultimately makes. This is because, as Aquinas says, 'the truth of the practical intellect depends on conformity with right appetite.'[75]

How does one acquire the moral virtues? Although Aquinas recognizes that some people are better *disposed* towards acquiring the virtues from birth, their proper actualization is always the outcome of habituation. This involves doing a certain action repeatedly until the tendency to do that action becomes a settled disposition, or an 'impression' within the soul.[76] This is true with respect to both making things and doing things. The more patio decks one builds, the better one becomes at building them. The same holds true with respect to the acts that comprise the moral life. By doing the relevant sorts of actions over and over – or, more accurately, being prompted to do such actions by our parents and teachers when we are young – our characters become formed in various ways. If one is to become courageous and self-restrained, for example, then one will need to practice doing the kind of actions that bring emotions such as fear and desire under the direction of reason.[77] The more we do certain actions, the easier it becomes for us to do them, and the more pleasure we take in doing them. Gradually, such dispositions become ingrained in our characters, and assume, as it were, second natures.

Once one has acquired the virtues, then, one will be in a position to do the right thing consistently, readily and with pleasure.[78] Such conditions are crucial. if we are to count a person as virtuous. If someone is to be considered self-restrained and just, for example, then they must be the sort of person that consistently treats others fairly and places restrictions on their desires. In other words, we have to be able to depend on the fact that the person will do certain things regularly if we are going to call them virtuous. If I am a soldier, I want to know that my comrade does not just do brave things accidentally or occasionally, but that he can *always* be counted on to do brave things. I also need to know that he does them because he wants to and does such actions unhesitatingly; otherwise I will not count him a 'courageous' man, nor will I be able to depend on him during combat.

By insisting on the foregoing features of moral virtue, Aquinas is clearly distinguishing it from other character traits. There are many people, for example, who *appear* virtuous, but are not. Rather, they do the right thing, but are tempted to do what is wrong because their lower appetites are out of harmony with their moral principles. Although they end up choosing what reason recommends over the direction in which appetite is pulling them, they nonetheless experience inner friction and thus lack integrity in its most basic sense. This is a disposition associated with what Aquinas calls 'continence' (*continentia*).[79] Likewise there are moral agents who do the wrong thing under the influence of passion, but end up regretting it in the cold light of day, as it were, since at some level they have the right sort of moral knowledge. We often witness this perplexing character trait when we see rational agents, including ourselves, doing things that they know are bad for them, such as smoking tobacco and putting too much salt on their food. Aquinas calls it 'incontinence' (*incontinentia*), contemporary moral philosophers refer to it as 'weakness of will' or 'moral weakness', and it is a very common human condition.[80] Like the virtuous person, and unlike the vicious person, both of these character types have the right sorts of principles. However, the fact that their lower appetites tempt them to do what is wrong is a sign of inner turmoil, and thus of a less than optimal state that leads to diminished happiness.

Much of the foregoing account of the moral virtues is consistent with Aristotelian ethics. Where Aquinas parts company with Aristotle, and indeed the entire pagan tradition of virtue ethics, is in his insistence that there also exist a trio of theological virtues: namely, faith (*fides*), hope (*spes*) and charity (*caritas*).[81] He is also emphatic in his belief that the cardinal virtues, in addition to being naturally acquired, are also sometimes divinely infused.[82] What do such infused virtues add to the naturally acquired moral virtues? They direct rational beings, so Thomas thinks, not merely to our natural destiny of human happiness, but to a destiny that transcends this. Because moral agents are ordered to the supernatural end of perfect happiness as actualized in the beatific vision, Aquinas quite reasonably concludes that such direction, because its object is God, will require supernatural assistance.

CHAPTER 6

POLITICS

The inclusion of a chapter on the political beliefs of a thirteenth-century theologian at first sight requires explanation. While Aquinas may still have something useful to contribute to modern debates over the nature of the soul, cognition, and the good life, to mention but a few, his political philosophy must surely be antiquated. In some respects this assumption has merit. Few nowadays, even those who share Aquinas's religious commitments, would agree with his preference for monarchy as the ideal form of government, even by the virtuous, not to mention his attitudes regarding gender differences and to relations between believers and non-believers. Few moderns, for example, would approve of Thomas's beliefs that women were naturally inferior and best suited to procreation or that it would be acceptable to burn heretics at the stake.[1] Clearly with respect to some of his political views, Aquinas was a man of his age. Still, in other respects, Aquinas had some highly relevant things to say about the nature of organized society, the need for social institutions such as government and the positive law, and whether or not war is ever justified.

THE FOUNDATIONS OF SOCIETY

Aquinas's views on the nature of social life were, as was so much of his thought in general, deeply influenced by Aristotle. William of Moerbeke's translation of Aristotle's *Politics* into Latin around 1260, meant that the West now had access to a conception of the foundations of society that was quite different from the ruling Augustinian model that had preceded it.[2] Henceforth, theoretical questions regarding the nature of authority both before and after the Fall, as well as those regarding the origins of the state, could take a more naturalistic or Aristotelian orientation, a more theological or Augustinian one, or could consist of an attempt to combine the two traditions. Aquinas's ideas on the foundations of society can best be seen as belonging to the third type, drawing as they do on both the Augustinian and the Aristotelian traditions.

For Aquinas, as for Aristotle, the state is a product of nature. This is manifest, and indeed emerges from the fact that man is a gregarious creature, or as Aquinas puts it, 'a social and political animal' (*animal sociale et politicum*). Man is therefore inclined by nature to live in communities for the purposes of survival and the attainment of the end to which he is directed: peaceful living and self-perfection. Reason teaches human beings that they have an end, and that the means to this end is communal life.[3] According to Aquinas, then, man's capacity to form associations with his fellows is a consequence of his instinct to survive. While prudence tells him that self-preservation is a basic good – that indeed it is a moral obligation according to the prescriptions of the natural law – it also shows him that, whereas other creatures are physically equipped for survival against the elements, man enters the world in a position of extreme vulnerability. For while nature has provided the lower animals with fur, horns and other attributes to aid them in the process of survival, man is born naked, helpless and dependent to a much greater extent than any other animal on the beneficence of others. Fortunately, he compensates for his natural shortcomings by the possession of reason and by his gregarious inclination. Accordingly, he naturally comes together with his fellows to form a community (*multitudo*) for the purposes of sociability and common protection, after which time a division of labour is effected.

Now, as Aristotle noticed, there is frequently a correlation between the size of a society and its living standard. The bigger a society is, the more advanced its standard of living. This is why the state, which is composed of many families and villages, is superior to the single family or village taken on its own. Aquinas agrees with this. If I live on my own, or just with my family, effectively isolated from any larger community, then I must obviously rely on myself for my basic needs. I must cook for myself, hunt for myself, farm for myself and heal myself and my family when we get sick. Needless to say, I may be able to learn how to do all of these things, but I will never learn to do them all as well as if I were just to focus on perfecting one skill. This obviously holds true for everyone else, which is why larger societies that allow for a division of labour contribute not just to the suste-nance of life, but to the good life. In larger societies, some people can devote a much greater share of their time to husbandry or medicine, thus becoming highly skilled and efficient at such activities, while others can likewise devote themselves to any number of other profes-sions, disciplines and trades. The result is an increase in knowledge and expertise, which can be accumulated and passed on to succeed-ing generations, thus resulting in an increase in the society's standard of living. As Thomas puts it: 'It is necessary that man live in larger communities so that each one may assist his fellows, and different men may be occupied in seeking, by their reason, to make different [discoveries] – one, for instance, in medicine, one in this and another in that.'[4]

Further evidence of man's social and political disposition, that is, of his natural inclination to form human associations, is *locutio*: the possession of speech. On Aquinas's view, as indeed on Aristotle's, humans alone of all the animals are endowed with the ability to speak, a mode of communication which is linked to their possession of reason, and which therefore permits them to think in abstract, universal terms and to share their thoughts with one another. This mode of communication also allows them to pass on the accumu-lated wisdom of their ancestors to successive generations. The lower animals, of course, do not have this capacity. Their mode of cogni-tion is limited to what they can perceive through their senses, and their ability to communicate with others is correspondingly rudimen-tary. This is the great divide, then, between humans and animals. Whereas the lower species can communicate to one another only through their most immediate emotions and desires, such as hunger and fear, human beings can apprehend and express abstract concepts, which in turn contribute to the material and moral progress of human societies.

For Aquinas, there are three types of human association, as we intimated a moment ago: the household (*familia*), the village (*vicus*) and the state (*civitas*). All three forms of association are natural. However, the measure of perfection of each is contingent on the degree to which it is self-sufficient. Because the *civitas* is most self-sufficient insofar it encompasses the family and the village, it is, so Thomas thinks, the most perfect. The state also represents the highest form of human association because it is not merely ordered towards life and its continuation, as is the family, but towards the virtuous life.[5] We will elaborate on this in the following section. For the time being, it is useful to see how Aquinas transformed the parameters of the debate over the foundations of society and the need for political authority from the strictly Augustinian paradigm that had been predominant.

Although Augustine's explicit treatment of the scope, nature and justification of political authority is relatively brief, he is generally held to believe two related things about the institution of government: (1) that it is essentially coercive, and (2) that it is a punishment for sin.[6] These features follow from Augustine's view of human nature. Since the Fall, human beings are burdened with the stain of original sin, a mode of existence characterized by self-love and its resulting tendency to elevate the objects of cupidity and sensual desire above the true good of submitting one's will to God. The existence of original sin makes the present life a continual struggle against the evils of promiscuity, vanity, temptation and wickedness, to mention only a few.[7]

Now, we can only be rescued from this miserable condition, so Augustine thinks, by divine assistance. God did not intend that human beings should have power over one another, much less that they should sin. He did create them with the freedom to choose between love of the world and love of himself, however, as part of the greater good. Unfortunately, such freedom entails that human beings have the capacity to do wrong, which makes the establishment of the state as an instrument of coercion necessary. That humans must submit themselves to political authority, with its monopoly on the means of violence, is a punishment for sin. As Augustine puts it: 'this subservience [to political authority] is penal and is ordained by that law which assists in preserving the natural order and forbids its disturbance; for if nothing had been done against that law, there would have been nothing to restrain by that subservience.'[8] For Augustine, if human beings are going to have even a minimally workable social existence, then, they require the imposition of a coercive authority to keep their selfish, anti-social tendencies in check.

To those who reject the notion of original sin and its implications for society, the Augustinian conception of political authority will seem unjustified. Indeed, many moderns will agree with the claim, famously articulated by the eighteenth-century philosopher Jean-Jacques Rousseau (1712–1778), that human beings are fundamentally good, and indeed perfectible, a view originally grounded in the belief that they possess an innate 'capacity for self-perfection' (*la faculté de se perfectionner*).[9] Indeed, Rousseau holds not only that individual humans are capable of moral progress, but that the entire *species* is perfectible.[10] What actually corrupts people, on this view, is not an innate tendency towards selfishness, avarice and malice. Rather, it is the formation of society, which creates competition for positional goods, and its institutions. The Augustinian view, of course, is the precise opposite. Social institutions are civilizing mechanisms that exist precisely to curb the anti-social tendencies that are innate to man. On the Rousseauian, social-constructivist view, by contrast, institutions are merely mechanisms by which social elites deprive the vulnerable of power.

Aquinas holds a somewhat more moderate and arguably more realistic view than the two foregoing extremes. He agrees with Augustine that humans are inherently subject to original sin, but he grants to political authority a much wider scope than merely to keep anti-social desires in check. Rather, he also regards as at least one of the functions of political authority and government to lead its citizens to virtue. This is because he grants, in contrast to Augustine, the possibility that a true, albeit diminished form of human self-perfection is achievable in the present life. He believes, then, that government and authority are not *merely* a punishment for sin. Recall that, if humans had not sinned, according to Augustine, then there would have been no need for political authority. This is not true for Aquinas. Even if humans *were* naturally good and perfectible, as Rousseau held, humans would *still* need government. Why? Aquinas cites two reasons for this: (1) to solve collective action problems and (2) for paternalistic reasons.

First, whenever human beings live in a community, they need some directive principle, so Thomas thinks, to attend to the common good.[11] The members of the community need not be prone deliberately to acting in anti-social ways in order for government to be necessary. Each person merely has to pursue his own good, as humans are inclined to do, for collective action problems to occur. That is, human beings are inclined – according to the model of human action to which Aquinas subscribes – to act in prudential, rational ways. By virtue of the fact that we have wills – inclinations to the good as apprehended by reason – we always do what we think will be good for us. Due to this, even in cases where there is no malice intended, the fact that each of us is pursuing our own interests usually has the effect of collectively undermining the common good which, para-doxically, undermines our *own* good. The solution to such problems is for each of us to agree to follow the laws of a legitimate authority to restrict our freedoms. In this way, we are all better off. This is why, for example, it is rational for societies to have rules of the road and authorities to enforce them. It is also why it is rational for us to *want* to have such rules. Without laws restricting everyone's behaviour while driving – although in the short term we would enjoy the appar-ent advantage of being able to drive how we like without threat of sanction – we would all be worse off in the long run. This is because everyone *else* would have the freedom to drive however they liked as well. The result would be chaos. One would not be able to get into one's car without risking life and limb, and this would obviously *not* be in our interests.

The second reason that political authority would be necessary, even if humans lacked an innate disposition to do wrong, has to do with an appeal to paternalism. According to Aquinas, if some people were naturally superior in practical wisdom and integrity to others, it would be unethical for the former not to use their talents to help others in achieving their final end.[12] This, of course, is a type of paternalism: the policy of the state, or someone in a position of authority, intervening in the affairs of another person for their own welfare, happiness or benefit. Of course, all agree that adults should act paternalistically towards children. This is because children have not yet accumulated the sort of wisdom or life experience that is nec-essary for them to make decisions that will benefit them in the long run. Children tend to think, that is, in terms of instant gratification. As applied to other adults, however, the practice of paternalism is nowadays considered controversial. If I want to smoke, for example, ride a motorcycle without a helmet, or engage in consensual dueling – legal prohibitions against which are usually considered forms of paternalism – then why should the state infringe on my freedoms as an autonomous adult and prevent me from doing such things?

The standard contemporary argument in favour of paternalism is that it does not really infringe on our freedoms. When the state forces us to do things for our own welfare, or prevents us from doing things that are not in our long-term interests, it is only making us do what we would want to do anyway if we were being fully rational. According to this view, when I smoke I am not being fully rational. Rather, I am under the influence of an irrational passion, which distorts my ability to make the right choice. Were I *not* under this passion, and thinking in a clear, rational way, I would refrain from smoking on the grounds that it is very bad for me. On this view, when the state places restrictions on smoking for the benefits of its citizens, it is getting some sort of hypothetical consent from the would-be smoker, and therefore not really doing anything against his or her will properly speaking.[13] Not everyone agrees with this justification.

We have to be cautious about attributing contemporary concerns to thinkers such as Aquinas. For one thing, Aquinas was not a modern liberal and therefore did not always have the same sorts of philosophical worries. Paternalism is controversial today because it is seen by some to conflict with modern notions of human agency, autonomy and subjective fulfilment, which were simply not Aquinas's concerns. Nonetheless, what Aquinas *does* have in common with contemporary defenders of paternalism is the view that rational agents ought to do what is in their long-term interests, and that sometimes the government, if it is wise and virtuous, can contribute towards their moral perfection. This stands to reason in the case of Aquinas. If there is an objective, human good, as Thomas thinks there is, then it follows that fallen beings, rational though they are, should be assisted in achieving it.

Now, Aquinas was well aware that governments can come in different forms, and he allowed for the possibility that different types of regime could be legitimate. In his little work, or opusculum, *On the Governance of Rulers* (*De Regno*), for example, he endorsed the view that monarchy, or the rule of a virtuous king, is the best form of government, a view partly informed by Neoplatonic ideas which regarded the universe, and by extension human society, as hierarchically ordered.[14] In the *Summa theologiae*, however, Thomas appears to prefer a mixed constitution in which the people, the aristocracy and the monarchy have a share in ruling.[15] Thomas's lack of consistency on this point may plausibly be explained by looking at the respective purposes of these two works. Whereas the *Summa* was a textbook intended for the training of young theologians, the *De regno* is an instance of the so-called 'mirror of princes' (*speculum principis*) genre of medieval writing. That is, the latter is essentially an instruction manual intended to advise medieval rulers, and was in fact dedicated to the King of Cyprus.[16] Each work should be read in light of their respective contexts. Despite these differences, however, it is important to recognize that Thomas is consistent in his belief that if a regime is to be considered legitimate, it must always rule with a view to the common good.

Nonetheless, we should bear in mind that when Aquinas refers to 'the people' having some share in government – as when he advocates for a mixed constitution in the *Summa theologiae* – we should not think that he is referring to 'the people' in our modern sense of the term. When modern liberal democrats argue that the people should rule themselves, they usually mean that – at least in representative democracies that are the norm in most Western democracies – each individual citizen of the age of majority has a say in who will represent them in the legislature of the country. This is very different from older forms of democracy, such as the classical republican model, in which citizens alternate with each other in the practice of ruling. Unlike representative democracies, such as exist today, these may be called *direct* or *participatory* democracies, because citizens do not simply vote, but take turns holding public office. Such models as the latter are possible in smaller-scale communities, as in ancient Athens or in the city-states of Renaissance Italy, but are probably unworkable in modern, large-scale nations. Although Aquinas was familiar with the concept of direct, participatory democracy from his reading of Aristotle, when he refers to 'the people' he almost certainly has in mind participation by corporate groups, as opposed to our understanding of 'one person, one vote.'[17]

Aquinas recognizes six possible types of political constitution, three of which meet the demands of justice, while the other three do not. Monarchy, aristocracy and polity signify the rule of the one, the few, and the many, respectively, who govern with a view to the common good. Because of this, these are all what we might call legitimate forms of political authority. By contrast, tyranny, oligarchy and what Aquinas sometimes calls 'democracy', signify the rule of the one, the few, and the many insofar as they govern, not with a view to common good, but in their own interests. Such forms of government are illegitimate.[18]

How should citizens respond to tyrannical regimes that abuse their power? While they are under an obligation to obey legitimate rulers, they are not similarly under an obligation, so Thomas thinks, to obey tyrants. Where a regime is legitimate, sedition against it is a grave sin, since to engage in such a practice is to undermine justice and the common good.[19] But where the regime rules not in the interests of the common good, and indeed subverts it by enacting unjust laws, Aquinas implies that it is licit to overthrow such a tyrannical regime, since this would not, strictly speaking, qualify as sedition. Indeed, if anyone is guilty of sedition in such a context it is the tyrant who 'spreads discord and division among the people under him so as to control them more easily'.[20] In doing so, the tyrant deliberately harms the community and undermines the common good. Needless to say, such regimes are usually ordered to the achievement and maintenance of the power and wealth of a select person or group. They therefore violate justice and indeed the very raison d'etre of large scale communities, which is to lead its citizens to virtue.

THE INSTITUTION OF HUMAN LAW

Societies or large-scale communities cannot exist without social institutions, the purpose of whose existence is to orient citizens towards the common good. Human beings are intrinsically social for Thomas, as we saw above, and indeed have 'a certain aptitude to virtue' (*quaedam aptitudo ad virtutem*).[21] However, rational agents are also self-interested beings subject to original sin who, if they do not have the proper socialization, will fail to realize that their individual good is tied up with the common good and end up pursuing the former to the exclusion of the latter. In the absence of virtues such as justice, they will accordingly set about making choices that undermine the interests of the community.[22]

The first and most basic institution that exists for the socialization of human beings is, of course, the family. Where the bonds of this social unit are strong, the children that arise from the sexual union of a man and a woman will usually be appropriately socialized. However, it sometimes happens that parents fail properly to habituate their children into being civic-minded, with the result that the child fails to internalize the habit of realizing that his interests are just one set among many, and to the extent that he must live in society, must learn how to voluntarily place restrictions on his desires. In instances where such habituation and parental admonition fail, or with those who are 'not easily responsive to words', as Thomas puts it, then the law will eventually have to intervene to enforce control by means of external constraint. In other words, it will be necessary for such individuals

> to be restrained from evil by force and fear, so that they might desist from wrong-doing, and leave others in peace, and that they themselves, by being habituated in this way, might be brought to do willingly what up to now they did from fear, and thus become virtuous. Now, this kind of training, which compels through fear of punishment, is the discipline of laws. Therefore in order that humans might have peace and virtue, it was necessary that laws be posited.[23]

Now, the foregoing quote is instructive, for it suggests that the purpose of human law is not merely to suppress anti-social inclinations, on Thomas's account, but additionally to lead citizens to some sort of virtue. But what *sort* of virtue? Does he envision the establishment of morality police, as it were, whose job is to enforce laws that will *coerce* people into becoming, not just law-abiding, but *good*? To see what Aquinas has in mind by this claim it will be illuminating to compare him to a very different, and to many people compelling, modern-day approach to the law and its limits: that of John Stuart Mill (1806–1873), an extremely influential architect of modern political thought.

According to Mill, the state and its public institutions do not exist to make men good. This is because, were the law to attempt to do this, it would violate the autonomy of its citizens.[24] This variant of liberalism is commonly known as 'anti-perfectionism'.[25] On this view, no one knows better, nor indeed cares more about what is best for me, than I do. Moreover, if the state just leaves me to my own devices, as it were, and allows me to make the sort of choices that *I* decide will best contribute to my welfare, the outcome will be the greatest happiness for the greatest number of people. This is because a society whose citizens are granted a maximum amount of personal freedom will be better able to generate the conditions in which rational agents can actualize their human potential and create something new and original in the world: themselves.

But if each of us is pursuing our own individual happiness without concern for the common good, will this not lead to the disintegration of society? To the contrary, for the Millian liberal, such conditions actually serve the common good, understood here as the aggregate of individual goods. This is because a society of contented rational agents each pursuing their own vision of what is valuable is more cohesive than a society of frustrated citizens who resent being infantilized by the state. Moreover, a society that allows individualism to flourish generates the conditions in which artistic and scientific geniuses, who elevate the aesthetic and material standards of the culture, are able to emerge.[26] On this account, a society of free men is much happier and progressive than those – such as one finds in traditional, tribal cultures – which enforce strict conformity to social norms as a means of public order and group cohesion.

Put otherwise, the liberal state, as Mill understands it, professes to be *neutral* with respect to the good. To the extent that the state uses the law as an instrument to enforce judgements of value about the private choices of its citizens, the positive law exceeds its proper scope, which lies solely in its ability to prevent or circumscribe harm.[27] So long as a citizen is not interfering with the rights of others to pursue their own conception of the good, then it is not the state's business to tell them how to lead their lives.[28] What, then, of people who make private choices that most would regard as immoral or distasteful? For Mill, if someone is racist, gossipy or backbiting, then polite society has its own sanctions: it will shun them. This is sufficient sanction. The modern liberal state, and the laws that it generates, in short, ought not to be in the business of perfecting people.

Now, we saw in the foregoing section that Aquinas is a type of paternalist. He regards it as quite licit for those in positions of political authority – so long as they are wise and virtuous – to assist those of their subjects who are less gifted in these respects to achieve their final end. A liberal such as Mill cannot really endorse this type of perfectionism since he rejects the notion that there is a good that is independent of individual desire.[29] Although Mill might agree to some extent with Aquinas's claim that happiness consists in self-development – which Mill thinks is best achieved in pluralistic liberal democracies – he cannot give such a notion the sort of content that Aquinas does. Mill's account of happiness, then, turns out to be rather thin compared to Aquinas's much richer account, since if Mill were to endorse a more substantive account of happiness, this would undermine his claim that personal choice is the paramount value. Mill is therefore a subjectivist and an anti-perfectionist, while Aquinas is an objectivist and a perfectionist.[30] But this still leaves us with the question of what sort of perfectionism Aquinas does actually endorse, and what role he sees human, positive law playing it its achievement.

For Aquinas, law is always, by definition, a command that is ordered to the common good. This holds as true of the eternal law as it does of the natural law or the positive law. If some rule or directive is not ordered to this end, but to only the private good of the ruler, then it is not truly a law but a parody or perversion of law.[31] But what precisely does Aquinas mean by the 'common good', a term which is, although frequently used by Aquinas, surprisingly vague? In one sense, of course, the common good is God, who is the beginning and end of all creatures insofar as they proceed from the Creator and return to him at the end of time.[32] But what we really want to know in this context is what it means as applied in a secular sense, that is, as the end of the political community and of human, positive law, as opposed to the theological end of all things.

At first sight, Aquinas's lack of clarity with respect to defining the common good (*bonum commune*) as compared to his rigor in defining the individual good is surprising since, in his commentary on Aristotle's *Politics*, he refers to the common good as the highest and most perfect good in human affairs.[33] Accordingly, such an end supersedes and takes priority over the good of the individual. Usually, and somewhat frustratingly, when Aquinas refers to the *bonum commune*, he neglects to define its essential features, preferring instead to merely provide some example or other of such an end.[34] The problem is further complicated by the fact that Aquinas seems to use the term equivocally. It was for this reason that the great German scholar Ignatius Eschmann remarked in the last century: 'The Thomistic notion of the common good is an analogical and very elusive notion.'[35]

One understanding of the common good that can safely be ruled out for Aquinas is the liberal definition according to which the common good refers to something like an aggregate of individual goods. As one contemporary commentator has put it: 'In a liberal society, the common good is the result of combining preferences, all of which are counted equally.'[36] On this view, the common good is not a fixed standard according to which individuals' preferences are measured but, on the contrary, an aggregate or pattern of their choices, which changes as their preferences change. If the majority in a political community comes to think it unfair to deny same-sex couples the right to marry, for example, then the common good, understood as such, demands that the law be changed to bring it into accordance with the peoples' altered preferences. Clearly this is a very subjective understanding of the common good. Since Aquinas is not a subjectivist, as we have seen, we can safely rule out his being committed to such a definition. To grasp what Aquinas has in mind when he refers to the *bonum commune*, it is perhaps useful to revisit his understanding of the individual good, and use this as a basis to infer, by analogy, what he means by the common good.

In the previous chapter, we saw that the individual good for Aquinas signifies happiness, by which he means the perfection or flourishing of the agent. Now, if beings such as ourselves are to flourish we must lead, so Thomas thinks, virtuous lives, which he sees as being closely bound up with rational perfection. Hence, 'the good of a human being *qua* human being is to have reason perfected for knowing the truth and the lower appetites governed by the rule of reason. For a human being is human precisely by being rational.'[37] Now, isolated acts of virtue do not qualify someone being counted as having a virtuous character, since almost anyone, including weak-willed and vicious people, are capable of acting morally from time to time. Rather, for an agent to be considered genuinely virtuous, he must show consistency of right action, knowledge that it is right, and a ready willingness to do the action should the circumstances demand. The virtuous agent must, as Aquinas puts it, be 'disposed to work towards the good in a good manner, that is, willingly, readily, with pleasure, and also reliably'.[38] A person who accidentally performs a virtuous action or is unaware that such an action corresponds to right reason cannot be called a virtuous person.

Now, every act of virtue performed by the agent can be said to contribute to his flourishing as a human being, while every act that is contrary to virtue or right reason detracts, so Thomas thinks, from his objective flourishing. This is why human happiness, at least in the present life, is not a state but an activity consisting in the disposition to do acts that are in accordance with right reason. As Aquinas says, 'man achieves [happiness] by many types of actions which are called merits; which is why, according to the Philosopher, happiness is the reward of virtuous conduct.'[39]

To extrapolate from the foregoing we can infer that, to the extent that the individual good signifies the flourishing of the individual person, the common good will consist, by analogy, in the flourishing of the community or the *civitas*. Accordingly, actions that contribute to the well-being of society and its institutions will be virtuous to the extent they serve the common good. Acts that undermine those institutions, on the other hand, will detract from that good. This is what Aquinas means when he says that laws – and indeed all institutions, such as the family – must be oriented to the common good, and indeed, that the goal of human society just *is* the common good.

Given the foregoing, it is not difficult to appreciate why Aquinas regards justice (*iustitia*) as the supreme cardinal virtue.[40] Because it involves abstracting from one's own personal situation to take into account the interests of others, justice is, of all the virtues, closest to reason, which is an abstractive power, as we saw in Chapter 4. But Aquinas also attaches great significance to the virtue of justice because it is vital to civic cohesion. The cardinal virtues of temperance and fortitude are, one might say, self-regarding since they perfect the person who possesses them by shaping the lower appetites in ways that will lead to happiness. Justice, by contrast, is other-regarding. It is not located in the sense appetites, but rather in the will.[41] It is, as Aquinas puts it, 'the constant and perpetual will to render to each one that which is his right'.[42] Justice, in short, involves giving to others what is due to them. This quality differentiates it from the other virtue that is located in the will, namely, the theological virtue of charity (*caritas*), in that the latter involves giving to others from one's own wealth, whereas the former involves giving to others what is theirs by right (*ius*).

It is paramount, then, if a society is to flourish, that it have citizens who possess at least a general orientation to the common good, a virtue Thomas calls 'legal justice', or what we might think of as civic-mindedness.[43] A citizenry that avoids paying taxes, for instance, clearly lacks the virtue of legal justice, because their actions detract from the flourishing of the societies to which they belong and undermine the public institutions that make any semblance of a good life possible for its citizens. In other words, a society in which individuals do not have a shared notion of the common good and are therefore unwilling to contribute to such an end will necessarily be a fragile one. This is because without such institutions as the army, the police and the judiciary, it will be difficult, if not impossible, to sustain an ordered society in which average, law-abiding people are able to go about the business of actualizing their human potential. Likewise, those who fail to observe the natural law injunction to reproduce detract from the common good, since well-organized societies must rely on its citizens to protect the community in times of war and, indeed, to pay the taxes that support its public institutions and physical infrastructure. In short, societies that cease to replace their populations in sufficient numbers, and whose citizens instead opt to orient their time and income towards individual self-fulfilment to the exclusion of the common good, will necessarily lose their tax base. The result is that such societies will become poorer and weaker. This failure of a citizenry to internalize an orientation to the common good was, of course, at least one important reason for the decline of Greece in antiquity and later of Imperial Rome. As the Greek historian Polybius (*ca.* 203–120 BC) complained of his age: 'In our time all Greece was visited by a dearth of children and a general decay of population. This evil grew upon us rapidly, and without attracting attention, by our men becoming perverted to a passion for show and money and the pleasures of idle life.'[44] It is also the reason that the Roman emperor Augustus, as Suetonius (b. 69 AD) informs us, imposed a 'bachelor tax' on young Roman men who delayed or otherwise refused to assume the burdens of married life and the duties associated with it.[45]

We are now in a better position to see what Aquinas means when he says that the purpose of the positive law is 'to lead men to virtue'.[46] Aquinas does not believe that it is the business of the state to inculcate every virtue into its citizens. It cannot, for example, make them pious, faithful to their spouses or otherwise force them to become admirable human beings. Aquinas does not, therefore, envision the establishment of a state-sanctioned morality police whose job it is to root out vice. This is not because he is a proto-liberal who prefers his political authorities to refrain from making judgements about peoples' personal life-style choices. Rather, it is, for Aquinas, a simple matter of pragmatism: it is simply unreasonable for a political authority to expect *all* its subjects to be perfectly virtuous. Because human law, as a matter of justice, needs to be applicable to all citizens, it must be possible for the average citizen to obey the edicts that arise from it. The law must therefore refrain from setting the bar too low, as it were, but it must also avoid setting it so high that ordinary people will find themselves unable to discharge what it demands. Hence, 'human laws do not prohibit all vices from which the virtuous abstain, but only the more serious ones from which it is possible for most people to abstain and especially those that seriously threaten others, without the prohibition of which human society could not be preserved.'[47]

Of course, there is very little in the foregoing, on the face of it, anyway, to which a liberal such as John Stuart Mill would object. Indeed, the job of the law for the modern liberal – its *only* job, as far as Mill is concerned – is to prevent the sort of harm to others that Aquinas describes in the aforementioned quote. When Aquinas argues elsewhere that it is the law's job to make people virtuous, then, does he have in mind that it should merely give them incentive to follow what contemporary philosophers call the Principle of Nonmaleficence, that is, to not do any harm? If this is all Aquinas means, then his conception of the sort of public virtue that it is legitimate for the state to encourage is as thin, or at least as modest, as Mill's.

But in fact Aquinas has a much richer account of the function of law and its relation to the common good. While a legitimate authority cannot expect its citizens to be perfectly virtuous, and therefore ought not to enact laws that it is impossible for most of them to obey, it has the right to expect its citizens to possess and exhibit the virtue of civic-mindedness or 'legal justice'. It is for this reason that Aquinas cites Aristotle approvingly when he writes: 'in order to be a good citizen, you need to love the good of the city. Now, if someone is allowed to share in the good of some city, he becomes its citizen and needs certain virtues for doing what a citizen does, and for loving the good of that city.'[48] And where citizens do not possess the pertinent civic virtues, it is appropriate for a political authority to use the law as an instrument to help orient them towards the common good.[49] A legitimate authority should, in short, enact laws that help to sustain the social institutions and practices without which order and, in general, a good life is impossible. We can therefore expect the laws, in a well-ordered Thomistic society, to be based on the natural law, and therefore oriented not just to sustaining life in all its forms, but even towards the promotion of the good life. Incentives to marry and to have children, the banning of suicide and infanticide, and restrictions on abortion could all be expected to be enshrined in law, then, in the ideal Thomistic society.[50] We could also expect, as part of what it means to be a good citizen, a respect, not just for basic social institutions such as the family, but for such public institutions as the church, the law and the academy, without which a civilized existence is all but impossible.

At this point a question naturally arises. Is Thomas an individualist and philosophical egoist, for whom the good life consists in self-perfection as we saw in the previous chapter? Or is Aquinas a communitarian? Put otherwise, what takes priority here, the individual citizen or the common good? The answer is that the individual good and the common good are in a sense inseparable for Aquinas given the nature of man, which is intrinsically social. Like Aristotle, Aquinas believes that, as intrinsically social beings, humans can only achieve the good life in a well-ordered society. Such a goal requires that citizens have a shared notion of the common good and be willing to contribute to it. At the same time, the common good is only a worthwhile end because it in turn contributes to the perfection of individuals by creating the conditions that make it possible for the citizens of a community to realize their full, human potential. In other words, the flourishing of the community that is associated with the common good cannot really be understood separately from the flourishing of individuals. The common good, then, takes priority over the individual not in the sense that it is the complete end of human life. Rather, it does so in the sense that individuals can only really flourish – in a secular, political sense, at any rate – when they devote at least some of their attention to the good of their communities and fellow citizens.

JUST WAR THEORY

Given the emphasis that Christianity places on love and non-violence, one might have expected Aquinas to defend some form or other of pacifism. After all, did Jesus not exhort his followers, when wronged by those who do evil, 'to turn the other cheek' (Matt: 5:38–42)? While there is undoubtedly a pacifist strain within certain forms of Christianity, it is equally true that, according to the natural law, rational creatures have an obligation to defend and preserve their lives. This will mean that, according to Christian thinkers such as Aquinas, it is sometimes justified for people to use violence against one another. Indeed, it will sometimes be justified for a society to employ the ultimate form of violence – war (*bellum*) – in order to preserve the security without which it will be impossible for citizens to pursue a good life. However, this right to use violence and to go to war must be strictly circumscribed. Aquinas was certainly not the first to think about what conditions must obtain if the violence that we call war is to be justified, but he was one of the better-known Christian thinkers, along with Augustine, who had a profound influence on the later development of just war theory.[51]

In the Western tradition, there have traditionally been three general attitudes to war, or what a recent commentator has defined as the 'actual, intentional and armed conflict between political communities'.[52] Of these three, two are radically opposed to one another, and the third occupies a median position between the two. The two extreme and radically-opposed views are generally known as *realism* and *pacifism*. The moderate position is known as *Just War Theory*. It is to this last tradition that Aquinas belongs. Before we can understand Thomas's attitude to war, however, it will perhaps be well to take a brief look at the alternatives.

Realism states that moral categories cannot be applied to affairs between nations. This position is usually associated with political voluntarism, which essentially holds that moral ascriptions simply arise from the will of a strong authority. Why is some action or policy right or wrong? Because it is against the law. Why is it against the law? Because the lawgiver has willed it thus. In the absence of a strong authority to make and enforce laws, there is simply anarchy, but there is no 'justice' or 'injustice' per se. Rather, there is merely the rights of radically self-interested individuals to do whatever are required to preserve themselves. Prudence, of course, recommends that rational individuals leave this so-called 'state of nature' and establish a strong civil authority to frame and enforce laws that place restrictions of the freedom of all members to harm one another. Once a civil authority is established that makes such laws, only then can we begin to talk about 'justice' and 'injustice'.

Now, notice what the foregoing position implies. If justice and injustice are relative to the will of a strong authority, then in the absence of such an authority, such terms are meaningless. Realists argue that this is in fact the case with respect to international relations, and are therefore highly sceptical that such language is applicable to this realm. Both individuals and nations act out of self-interest, on this view, and there is nothing in principle wrong with that. However, when an individual who belongs to a civil society or a legal jurisdiction finds himself in a dispute with another individual, he can take his dispute to an independent judge who can arbitrate. However, in the case of international disputes, according to the realist, there *is* no independent arbiter or judge that can peacefully settle the dispute. Rather, there is only war.[53]

The best-known defender of realism and voluntarism with respect to political authority is, historically speaking, Thomas Hobbes (1588–1679), although this position goes well back into antiquity. Indeed, one of the most famous articulations of the realist position occurs in the so-called Melian Dialogue of Thucydides (*ca.* 460–395 BC), which occurs in his *History of the Peloponnesian War*. The Dialogue chronicles – or purports to do so, anyway – a famous episode during the war between Athens and Sparta from 431 BC to 404 BC. Athens had surrounded the island of Delos, an ally of Sparta's, and proceeded to send a delegation to the much weaker island. The point was to offer the citizens of Delos an ultimatum: either surrender to the will of the Athenians, become one of its colonies and have their lives spared, or be brutally conquered and killed or sold into slavery. The Melians, being far weaker and therefore unlikely to defeat the Athenians' militarily, appealed to abstract principles of justice and international law – at least in part – in an attempt to dissuade the Athenians from embarking on aggression against them. The Athenian delegation, by contrast, argued from the perspective of realism. On their view, '[n]ature always compels gods, we believe, and men, we are certain, to rule over anyone they can control. We did not make this law, and we were not the first to follow it; but we will take it as we found it and leave it to posterity forever, because we know that you would do the same if you had our power, and so would anyone else.'[54] What justifies war is not morality, but expedience. Where there is no powerful authority, there is no law. And where there is no law, there is no justice or injustice. Rather, there is only self-interest, particularly in relations between states.

Note that the Hobbesian conception of law is very different from the Thomistic view that we laid out in the previous chapter. On the Hobbesian conception – a crude and early version of legal positivism – law is any command or decree by a superior that can be backed up by the threat of force. Law thus reduces, essentially, to the arbitrary will of a lawgiver. Aquinas's view of law is very different. It is a command of *reason*, rather than will, which is directed to the common good. None of this is to imply that Thomas laid out a full-blown defense of international law such as we understand it today. The task of giving a robust defense of the need for international law would therefore have to wait for several centuries, when it was defended by such early-modern, natural law thinkers as Hugo Grotius (1583–1645), widely considered the 'father of modern international law'. Thomas did, however, have something to say about the morality of war, and he most certainly did influence thinkers such as Grotius in this regard.

Pacifism, by contrast, holds that moral categories can and should be applied to relations between states and that when it comes to war, there can never be moral justification. This is because, so the pacifist believes, there is always some alternative to going to war to settle disputes. But can this really be right? Suppose, the critic of pacifism might say, some power was to invade a neighbouring country in order to expand its territory. Would not the victims of such aggression have the right to resort to armed resistance to repel the invaders? Now, the pacifist concedes that it is morally justified to resist such aggression. What they reject is the claim that such resistance must necessarily take the form of *armed* resistance. For example, the pacifist might argue, the victims of aggression might strike or otherwise refuse to work for their new masters. Or they might organize demonstrations and rallies and, in general, resort to other forms of civil disobedience. This method was very effective in achieving justice for Ghandi and Martin Luther King Jr., so the pacifist will argue, why would it not be effective in other contexts?[55]

It has been pointed out, however, that the common tactics associated with non-violent resistance, such as were used by Ghandi and King, rely for their efficacy on the fundamental decency of the colonizing power. It is because the British, whatever their other faults, were sufficiently responsive to demands for justice that India gained its liberation through non-violence. Likewise in the case of Martin Luther King's demands for equality during the civil rights movement in the United States. But suppose that the invading power is Nazi Germany? Does anyone really believe, the non-pacifist will argue, that such a regime would have been similarly moved by such considerations? A likelier scenario is that they would have acted towards those they conquered much as the Athenians acted towards the Delians: either killed them or forced them into slave labour as a punishment for resisting. Indeed, this is precisely what the Nazis *did* do to those who resisted them.[56]

It is for this reason that pacifism has been criticized for being naïve and utopian. Others see it as being vulnerable to a more serious charge.

By opposing war outright, this critique goes, the pacifist gets to assume the moral high ground and keep his hands clean. At the same time, he gets to benefit from the safety that is provided by those of his compatriots who are willing to get their hands dirty, as it were, by employing violence to defend the community. The pacifist, in other words, is a free rider.[57] Whether this charge is fair or not, at the very least, one may agree with the famous contemporary philosopher John Rawls who regarded pacifism as an 'unworldly view'.[58]

Arguably, both realism and pacifism make the world a much more dangerous place. This is because both positions, in their own ways, reward aggression by providing nations that are inclined to such behaviour with incentive to exercise their power. Realism does this by implicitly endorsing the notion that might makes right, as it were, and pacifism by its principled unwillingness to confront evil and aggression with the threat of actual force. The result is that the realm of international relations becomes a lawless one that encourages nations, in the absence of laws that might protect them, to arm themselves in ways that ensure a Hobbesian race to the bottom. The only solution to such a state of affairs is to enact laws that restrict the ability of countries to exercise their military power, particularly when it comes to attacking others.

Between the two extremes of realism, which is sceptical of moral claims in the international arena, and pacifism, which generates moral stipulations that are arguably *too* demanding, there is the tradition of Just War Theory (JWT). According to this school of thought, although war can be morally justified, it is only so insofar as it meets several rigorous criteria. The JWT tradition therefore agrees with realism in its view that war is sometimes permissible, though it rejects the realist's moral scepticism. The fact of the matter is we *can* talk meaningfully about the morality and immorality of war. Some wars, however horrific and undesirable, *are* 'moral' or 'just,' while other wars are terribly 'immoral' or 'unjust'. Likewise JWT partly agrees with the pacifist, and partly disagrees with him. It agrees with the pacifist that morality is applicable to relations between states or kingdoms, although it rejects the pacifist's absolutist rejection of violence.

According to contemporary JWT, there are three ways of thinking about the morality of war: (1) *ius ad bellum*, which refers to the conditions that must be met in order to justify going to war, (2) *ius in bello*, which refers to the sort of moral conduct that soldiers in the field must observe while waging war, and (3) *ius post bellum*, or the rules and moral principles surrounding the termination of wars. Aquinas's thoughts on JWT are applicable only to criteria associated with *ius ad bellum* and possibly *ius in bello*. He has nothing to say about the moral requirements associated with terminating warfare, which is a more recent development of JWT. Aquinas is mainly concerned, then – as were most theorists who defended the morality of war before him and then into the early modern period – with formulating the principles that attach to declaring war, along with those that are associated with prosecuting it.

The relevant discussion of Aquinas's theory of just war in the *Summa* is to be found at II–II, q. 40, a. 1, which is part of the Treatise on the Theological Virtues. The context is interesting for a number of reasons. First, Thomas's treatment of war ironically forms part of a larger discussion on the theological virtue of love or charity (*caritas*). Second, Aquinas relies on authorities for his claims to a much greater extent that on almost any other topic. The first is perhaps easier to explain than the second. Charity is the divinely infused habit that, if possessed, generates love for God and love for other human beings for the sake of God. Needless to say, the practice of war, at first sight, seems completely antithetical to such a virtue. Why discuss war – and indeed other forms of social disruption as sedition and schism – in such a context? Although Aquinas does not explicitly argue this, his explanation would undoubtedly be that while we are obliged to love our neighbours, we are also under an obligation to defend ourselves and our communities, without the latter of which human life, not to mention love, would simply be impossible.

The second feature of Aquinas's discussion of war, that is, its excessive reliance on authority to defend his claims, is harder to explain. In the main body of the article and in his replies to the objections – the two places in each article where one typically finds Aquinas's own *arguments* for a certain position, as opposed to simply reporting the positions of others – we find him citing authorities no fewer than eleven times: eight times with respect to Augustine and Jerome, and three times with respect to scriptural authorities such as Matthew and Paul. Indeed there is very little in the way of *argument* at all in q. 40, a. 1. This is very unusual. Now, this is not meant to suggest that scholastic theologians such as Aquinas were uninterested in demonstrating their faithfulness to authority. On the contrary, one cannot fail to get the impression when reading Aquinas – or most other scholastics, for that matter – that he is keenly interested in demonstrating that his views harmonize with some great authority or another. It is just that Aquinas was also interested in *defending* his positions, generally using good arguments, which procedure seems virtually to have been abandoned in the present case. Just why this is so, we do not care to speculate.

In order that war be justified, according to Aquinas, three conditions must be met. First, the authority to declare war can only issue from a public person. Private citizens do not have the right to wage war. This is because when the right (*ius*) of a private citizen has been violated, he or she has recourse to a civil judge to settle the dispute peacefully.[59] The monopoly on violence and coercion, by contrast, must exclusively belong to the state, since if it did not, there would be discord, which would not serve the common good. In relations between states, however, there is no arbiter that can settle disputes or enforce any regulations. When a political entity believes that its rights have been violated, accordingly, it must go to war, the decision over which belongs to the authority that has care over the common good. Since the common good is defined, in its essence, as the ordering and flourishing of the community, one of the primary tasks of any legitimate authority is the defense of the community.

The second condition is that the *casus belli*, the cause of war, must be a just one. How does one determine a just or moral cause? Aquinas is vague on this particular point, stating only that 'those who are attacked should be attacked because they deserve it on account of some fault.'[60] The tradition of just war usually interprets the sort of 'fault' to which Aquinas is referring as some form of unjust aggression, where this takes the form of a violation of the basic rights of a group of people.[61] Now, whether a country is *only* justified in going to war for reasons of self-defense, or whether they may additionally go to war for humanitarian purposes, as we might say today, is unclear from what Aquinas claims. Based on his defense of the natural law precept for self-preservation, we may safely infer that at the very least, nations may go to war to defend themselves. But Aquinas also states that the punishing of evil-doers and the securing of peace are legitimate reasons for going to war.[62] Beyond that, Aquinas is silent on the question of whether it is ever licit to go to war in order to correct or influence the behaviour of a foreign population or ruler.[63] This is perhaps a controversial idea today.

The third condition that must be met is that the war must waged with a correct intention. As Aquinas puts it, the belligerents must 'intend the advancement of good or the avoidance of evil'.[64] In short, the authority waging war must be motivated by the reasons cited for the *casus belli*. For if his motivation is *really* vainglory, revenge or plunder, then he does not have a moral right to wage war.[65]

A final point that should be mentioned in the present context is what has come to be known as the Doctrine of Double Effect (DDE). This doctrine tends to regulate the part of JWT known as *ius in bello* since it mainly applies to the actual conduct of warfare. Put briefly, the DDE states that where an act has two effects, one good and one bad, the bad may be permitted so long as several conditions are met. First, the act must be good, or at least morally neutral. Second, the good effect must be intended, and the bad effect, although foreseen ahead of time, merely accidental. Third, the bad effect may not be the means to the good effect; and, fourth, the results achieved by the good effect must outweigh those of the bad.[66] The doctrine arises from a common intuition shared by many people, which holds that one of the salient features of the moral life is the existence of certain grey areas, as it were, and that sometimes it is impossible to achieve a good effect under certain circumstances without simultaneously causing something one regards as bad to happen. In short, it seems to lend articulation to the moral intuition that sometimes bad effects can be tolerated so long as they are unintended and do not outweigh the good that will result.

The DDE has become an enormously useful and influential principle in practical ethics, not just with respect to the waging of war, but in all circumstances where there is a crucial distinction to be made between *killing* and *allowing-to-die*, the former being, to most people, impermissible, while the latter is not. It therefore has applicability not only with respect to JWT in situations where it is impossible for soldiers to carry out legitimate military missions without killing innocent civilians, but in the field of medical ethics as well, and specifically with respect to the distinction between passive versus active euthanasia.

NOTES

1 INTRODUCTION

1 Gilson presents his view that Aquinas 'established the act-of-being as the keystone of metaphysics' in *The Christian Philosophy of St. Thomas Aquinas*, trans. L. K. Shook (Notre Dame, IN: University of Notre Dame, 1994), 368–75. Kenny first expressed his views in his introductory book *Aquinas* (Oxford: Oxford University Press, 1980), and gives fuller treatments in his *Aquinas on Mind* (London: Routledge, 1993) and *Aquinas on Being* (Oxford: Clarendon Press, 2002).

2 Lombard's *Sentences*, composed between 1154 and 1157, was an attempt at an organized, or 'systematic', theology, dealing with God as creator, the human being as a rational creature made in the divine image, and Jesus Christ as the union of God and man. Its matter included the opinions, or 'sentences' (*sententiae*), of various Church fathers, who had a formative influence on medieval Christian theology.

3 C. S. Lewis, *The Discarded Image* (Cambridge: Cambridge University Press, 1964), 10. Lewis quotes the saying without attribution.

4 See Aristotle, *Physics* book 8, chap. 1. For a brief summary of Aristotle's arguments against a beginning of things, see R. Sorabji, *Time, Creation, and the Continuum: Theories in Antiquity and the Early Middle Ages* (Ithaca, NY: Cornell University Press, 1983), 276–83.

5 See M. D. Jordan, 'Theology and Philosophy', in *The Cambridge Companion to Aquinas*, ed. N. Kretzmann and E. Stump (Cambridge: Cambridge University Press, 1993), 232–251; and Idem, 'The Alleged Aristotelianism of Thomas Aquinas', reprinted in *The Gilson Lectures on Thomas Aquinas* (Toronto: Pontifical Institute of Mediaeval Studies, 2008), 73–106.

6 This does not include the 'Supplement' to the Third Part, which includes material from Aquinas's much earlier commentary on the *Sentences*, added to fill out the questions Aquinas had planned to write but did not complete.

2 METAPHYSICS

1 On this topic, see J. Weisheipl, 'Classification of the Sciences in Medieval Thought,' *Mediaeval Studies* 27 (1965): 54.

2 I take this useful expression from A. Maurer's introduction to his translation of Aquinas's *Commentary on Boethius's De Trinitate* in *The Division and Methods of the Sciences*, 4th ed. (Toronto: Pontifical Institute of Mediaeval Studies, 1986), x.

3 Ibid.

4 See Aristotle's *Physics* book 2, chaps. 3–9 (194b16–200b9) and *Metaphysics* book 1, chaps. 3–10 (983a24–993a27).

5 See Aquinas, *On Being and Essence*, chap. 1.

6 Aquinas, *Commentary on the Metaphysics*, Proemium. In *The Division and Methods of the Sciences*, appendix 2, 96.

7 Aquinas, *Commentary on Boethius's De Trinitate*, q. 5, a. 4 corp.

8 Ibid.

9 Cf. ibid., 51.

10 See R. Stark, *The Victory of Reason: How Christianity Led to Freedom, Capitalism, and Western Success* (New York: Random House, 2005).

11 Aquinas, *Commentary on Boethius's De Trinitate*, q. 5, a. 4 corp.

12 For a clear treatment of the problem of evil and its solutions, see J. L. Mackie, *The Miracle of Theism: Arguments for and Against the Existence of God* (Oxford: Clarendon Press, 1982), 150–176.

13 C. Darwin, *Origin of Species by Means of Natural Selection* (New York: Modern Library, 1993).

14 The most famous defender of this sort of Darwinistic positivism is Richard Dawkins; cf. his *The God Delusion* (Boston: Houghton Mifflin, 2006).

15 For a defense of the view that the doctrine of original sin actually *led* to the search for certain knowledge, which in turn provided the foundations of modern science, see P. Harrison, *The Fall of Man and the Foundations of Science* (Cambridge: Cambridge University Press, 2007).

16 Cf. Aquinas, *Summa contra gentiles*, book 1, chap. 12.

17 For the history of this concept, see T. Carroll, 'The Traditions of Fideism,' *Religious Studies* 44 (2008): 1–22.

18 *Summa theologiae* (hereafter *ST*)I, q. 48, a. 1 corp.: ' . . . one opposite is known through the other, as darkness is known through light. Hence, also what evil is must be understood from the nature of good. Now, we said above that good is that which is desirable; and thus, since every nature desires its own being and its own perfection, it must also be said that the being and perfection of any nature is good. Hence, it cannot be the case that evil signifies any being, or any form or nature. It remains therefore that by the name of evil is signified the absence of good.'

19 *ST* I, q. 49, a. 1 corp.: ' . . . it must be said that every evil to some degree has a cause. For evil is the defect of good, which is natural and belongs to a thing. But that anything fail from its natural and proper disposition can come only from some cause drawing it out of its proper disposition. For a heavy thing is not moved upwards except by some impelling force; nor does an agent fail in its action except due to some impediment. But only good can be a cause, because nothing can be a cause except inasmuch as it is a being, and every being, as such, is good.'

20 *Summa Contra Gentiles*, Book 3, chap. 64.

21 Ibid., chaps. 55 and 56.

22 *ST* I, q. 2, a. 2 ad 3: '. . . From effects that are not proportionate to their cause, no perfect knowledge of that cause can be obtained. However, from every effect, the existence of the cause can be manifestly demonstrated. Thus the existence of God can be demonstrated from his effects, albeit from [these effects] we cannot perfectly know God as he is in his essence.'

23 Anselm, *Proslogion*, chap. 1: ' "Enter into the chamber" of your mind, shut out everything but God and whatever helps you to seek him, and seek him "behind closed doors". Speak now, my whole heart: say to God, "I seek your face; your face, Lord, do I seek." ' In Anselm, *Basic Writings*, trans. T. Williams (Indianapolis: Hackett, 2007), 79.

24 Ibid., 80.

25 Ibid., 79.

26 Ibid., chap. 2, 82.

27 Ibid., chap. 4: 'No one who understands what God is can think that God does not exist, although he may say these words in his heart with no signification at all, or with some peculiar signification.' (trans. Williams, 83).

28 Aquinas, *ST* I, q. 2, a. 1 ad 2: 'It is possible that not everyone who hears the word "God" understands it to signify "something than which nothing greater can be thought," given that some have believed that God is a body. However, granted that everyone understands that by this word "God" is signified "something than which nothing greater can be thought," nevertheless, it does not follow that he understands that what the word signifies actually exists, but only that it exists in the mind.'

29 *ST* I, q. 2, a. 3 corp.

30 Ibid.

31 Ibid.

32 Ibid.

33 J. Owens, 'Aquinas and the Five Ways,' in *St. Thomas Aquinas on the Existence of God: The Collected Papers of Joseph Owens*, ed. J. Catan (Albany: SUNY Press, 1980), 136.

34 *ST* I, q. 2, a. 3 corp.

35 *ST* I, q. 2, a. 2 corp.

36 Aquinas, commentary on the *Sentences*. Quoted in *An Aquinas Reader*, ed. M. Clark (New York: Image Books, 1972), 97.

37 Ibid.

38 Duns Scotus, *Ordinatio* I.3.1.1–2, n. 40. Quoted in R. Cross, *Duns Scotus* (Oxford: Oxford University Press, 1999), 36.

39 Duns Scotus, *Lectura* I.3.I. 1–2, n. 113: 'Unless "being" implies one univocal intention [i.e., concept], theology would simply perish. For theologians prove that the divine Word proceeds and is begotten by way of intellect, and the Holy Spirit proceeds by way of will. But if the intellect and will were found in us and in God equivocally, there would be no evidence at all that, since a word is begotten in us in such and such a fashion, it is so in God – and likewise with regard to love in us – because then intellect and will in these two cases would be of a wholly different kind [*ratio*]'. Quoted in Cross, 36.

40 Aquinas, *Summa Contra Gentiles* I, 32: 'An effect that does not receive a form specifically the same as that through which the agent acts cannot receive according to a univocal predication the name arising from that form. Thus the heat generated by the sun and the sun itself are not called univocally *hot*' (trans. A. Pegis, 143).

41 Ibid.: 'Now the forms of the things God has made do not measure up to a specific likeness of the divine power; for the things that God has made receive in a divided and particular way that which in Him is found in a simple and universal way. It is clear, then, that nothing can be said univocally of God and other things.'

42 *ST* I, q. 13, a. 5 corp.: 'Nor are names applied to God and creatures in a purely equivocal sense, as some have said. Because then nothing could be known or demonstrated about God, but the fallacy of equivocation would befall them. And this contradicts the philosophers, who demonstratively prove many things about God, and also contradicts what the Apostle says in *Romans* I, 20: "The invisible things of God are clearly seen being understood by the things that are made."'

43 Ibid.

44 Ibid.: 'Hence, whatever is said of God and creatures is said insofar as there is some relation of the creature to God as to its principle and cause, by which all the perfections of things pre-exist in an excellent way.'

45 *ST* I–II, q. 94, a. 2 corp.

46 Ibid., I, q. 3, a. 5 ad 1.

47 Ibid., I-II, q. 7, a. 1 corp.

48 Aquinas, *On The Principles of Nature*. In *An Aquinas Reader*, ed. Clark, 163–72.

49 *Summa contra gentiles,* book 2, chap. 54.

50 Aquinas, *On the Principles of Nature*, ed. Clark, 163.

51 *Summa contra gentiles*, book 2, chap. 53: "[W]hatever participates in a thing is compared to the thing participated in as act to potentiality . . . But . . . God alone is essentially a being, whereas all other things participate in being. Therefore, every created substance is compared to its own being as potentiality to act" (trans. J. F. Anderson, 156).

52 Cf. J. F. Wippel, 'Essence and Existence,' in *The Cambridge History of Later Medieval Philosophy*, ed. N. Kretzmann, A. Kenny and J. Pinborg (Cambridge: Cambridge University Press, 1982), 395.

53 *ST* I, q. 29, a. 2 ad 3.

54 *Summa contra gentiles*, book 1, chap. 22.

55 Aquinas, *On Being and Essence*, chap. 4 (trans. Maurer, 55). For a classic treatment of this, see L. Sweeney, 'Existence/Essence in Thomas Aquinas's Early Writings,' *Proceedings of the American Catholic Philosophical Association* 37 (1963): 97–131.

56 Ibid.: 'Whatever belongs to a thing is either caused by the principles of its nature (as the capacity for laughter in man) or comes to it from an extrinsic principle (as light in the air from the influence of the sun). Now being itself cannot be caused by the form or quiddity of a thing . . . because that thing would then be its own cause and it would bring itself into being,

which is impossible. It follows that everything whose being is distinct from its nature must have being from another. And because everything that exists through another is reduced to that which exists through itself as to its first cause, there must be a reality that is the cause of being for all other things, because it is pure being . . . and this is the first cause, or God' (trans. Maurer, 56–7).

3 PSYCHOLOGY

1 *ST* I, q. 75, a. 1 corp.: 'The philosophers of old, not being able to rise above their imagination, supposed that the principle of these actions was something corporeal: for they asserted that only bodies were real things; and that what is not corporeal is nothing. Hence, they maintained that the soul is some sort of body. This opinion can be proved in many ways to be false; but we shall make use of only one proof, which shows quite universally and certainly that the soul is not a body.'

2 See *ST* I, q. 75, a. 1 args. 1–3.

3 See *ST* I, q. 75, a. 4. This is a special kind of matter, which Aquinas calls 'common matter', to distinguish it from the matter found in individuals, which he calls 'designated matter' (*materia signata*).

4 *ST* I, q. 75, a. 2.

5 *ST* I, q. 75, a. 2 corp. For a critical discussion of this argument, see N. Kretzmann, 'Philosophy of Mind', in *The Cambridge Companion to Aquinas*, ed. N. Kretzmann and E. Stump (Cambridge: Cambridge University Press, 1993), 132–133.

6 For Descartes's mind-body dualism, see his *Meditations on First Philosophy*, especially Meditations 2 and 6. Descartes's strongest statement of the unity of the human being occurs in Meditation 6, the last in the work. He writes, 'By means of these sensations of pain, hunger, thirst and so on, nature also teaches not merely that I am present to my body in the way a sailor is present in a ship, but that I am most tightly joined and, so to speak, commingled with it, so much so that I and the body constitute one single thing' (trans. D. A. Cress [Indianapolis: Hackett, 1993], 53). Nevertheless, he continues to maintain to the end that 'the mind is wholly diverse from the body' (56).

7 In *ST* I, q. 76, a. 1 ad 4, Aquinas says that 'the human soul, by reason of its perfection, is not a form immersed in matter, or entirely embraced by matter. Therefore there is nothing to prevent some power from not being the act of the body, although the soul is essentially the form of the body.'

8 *ST* I, q. 76, a. 1 corp.: 'But if anyone says that the intellectual soul is not the form of the body, he must first explain how it is that this action of understanding is the action of this particular man; for everyone is conscious that it is he himself who understands.'

9 *ST* I, q. 76, a. 1 corp.

10 This mini-argument for the soul's incorruptibility appears at the end of the response to *ST* I, q. 75, a. 6, as a sort of corollary to the main

arguments Aquinas offers there. It is interesting enough to quote in full: 'Moreover, we may take a sign of this from the fact that everything naturally aspires to existence after its own manner. Now, in things that have knowledge, desire ensues upon knowledge. The senses indeed do not know being, except under the conditions of *here* and *now*, whereas the intellect apprehends existence absolutely, and for all time; so that everything that has an intellect naturally desires always to exist. But a natural desire cannot be in vain. Therefore, every intellectual substance is incorruptible.'

11 In addition to being aware of their own acts, intellect and will are also aware of the other's acts. As Aquinas puts it, 'these powers include one another in their acts, because the intellect understands that the will wills, and the will wills the intellect to understand' (*ST* I, q. 82, a. 4 ad 1).

12 *ST* I, q. 79, a. 1 ad 2

13 *ST* I, q. 79, a. 2 corp.

14 Aristotle, *De anima* book 3, chap. 4 (430a1): 'What it [thought] thinks must be in it just as characters may be said to be on a writing-table on which as yet nothing actually stands written: this is exactly what happens with thought.' Trans. J. A. Smith, in *The Complete Works of Aristotle*, ed. J. Barnes, 2 vols. (Princeton: Princeton University Press, 1984), vol. 1: 683.

15 *ST* I, q. 79, a. 2 corp.

16 *ST* I, q. 79, a. 3 corp.: 'We must therefore assign on the part of the intellect some power to make things actually intelligible, by abstraction of the species from material conditions. And such is the necessity for positing an agent intellect.'

17 *ST* I, q. 79, a. 2 ad 2: 'The intellect which is in potentiality to things intelligible, and which for this reason Aristotle calls the *possible intellect*, is . . . not an act of a corporeal organ.'

18 *ST* I, q. 79, a. 5 corp.

19 In *ST* I, q. 82, a. 1 corp., Aquinas gives the examples of food being necessary for life, a horse being necessary for a journey, and a ship being necessary to cross the ocean. In cases involving transportation, modern technology has multiplied the options beyond those which Aquinas could cite, but the philosophical point remains the same.

20 In *ST* I, q. 82, a. 1 corp., Aquinas distinguishes three different kinds of necessity: (1) natural necessity, which arises from intrinsic properties of a thing (e.g. triangles necessarily have three sides); (2) necessity of the end (e.g. food is necessary for life); and (3) necessity of coercion. The last is clearly incompatible with the will's voluntary activity, but the first two for Aquinas are not.

21 See *ST* I, q. 83, a. 3 corp.

22 *ST* I, q. 82, a. 3 corp.

23 See *ST* I, q. 82, a. 3 corp.

24 See *ST* I, q. 75, aa. 2 and 6 corp.

25 For example, in *Aquinas on Mind*, Kenny says that '[i]t was primarily on theological grounds that St Thomas believed in the possibility of an

afterlife for the soul after the death of the body. A philosopher who does not share these religious presuppositions will find it unrewarding to follow in detail the account given of the intellectual activity of the disembodied soul' (126).

26 Aquinas, *Super I ad Corinthios* 15.2: 'It is plain that a human being naturally desires his own salvation. But the soul, since it is a part of the human body, is not the whole human being, and my soul is not I. So even if the soul were to achieve salvation in another life, it would not be I or any human being.' Trans. R. Pasnau, in *The Treatise on Human Nature* Summa Theologiae *1a 75–89* (Indianapolis: Hackett, 2002), 411.

27 See *ST* I, q. 75, a. 2 corp., which begins: 'It must necessarily be allowed that the principle of intellectual operation, which we call the soul of man, is a principle both incorporeal and subsistent.' He goes on in article 6 of the same Question to consider whether the soul is corruptible (*corruptibilis*) or not.

28 These objections are introduced in the opening arguments of *ST* I, q. 75, a. 6, though in a different order from the one we present here.

29 *ST* I, q. 75, a. 6 corp.

30 See *ST* I, q. 77, a. 1 corp.; compare also *ST* I, q. 76, aa. 3 and 4.

31 *ST* I, q. 75, a. 6 corp.

32 Ibid.

33 See Aristotle, *De anima* book 3, chap. 4, which deals with 'that part of the soul (whether it is separable in extended space, or only in thought) with which the soul knows and thinks' (trans. Hett, 165). In the course of drawing out differences between perception and thinking, Aristotle notes that 'the faculty of sense is not apart from the body, whereas the mind is separable' (167).

34 In *ST* I, q. 89, a. 1 corp., Aquinas says that corporeal phantasms – images of things formed from sensory impressions – 'are in corporeal organs'. Phantasms are explained more fully in Chapter 4.

35 Ibid. 'In that case, however, the union of soul and body would not be for the soul's good, for evidently it would understand worse in the body than out of it; but the union would be for the good of the body, which would be absurd, since matter exists for the sake of the form, and not the form for the sake of matter.'

36 Ibid.

37 Aquinas uses a similar analogy in *ST* I, q. 89, a. 1 corp.

38 Ibid.

39 Aquinas stopped writing the *Summa theologiae* before he came to the question of the resurrection, which would have appeared in the Third Part. His views on the reunion of the soul and body can be found in his *Compendium of Theology*, chaps. 151–153, and his earlier work *Summa contra gentiles*, book 4, chaps. 79–81.

40 Aquinas, *Compendium of Theology*, chap. 153, trans. C. Vollert (St. Louis: Herder, 1947), 162.

41 Ibid.

4 EPISTEMOLOGY

1 *Epistēmē,* the Greek term for scientific knowledge, is translated into Aquinas's Latin as *scientia*. Questions 84–89 in the First Part of the *Summa theologiae* offer a systematic account of the process of knowledge, even if it is not comprehensive. The account in this chapter is largely based on those questions.

2 Aquinas cites Plato as the source of this view in *ST* I, q. 84, a. 1 corp., though he is criticizing Plato there for supposing that these conditions not only apply to the knower, but to the thing known. Hence, Plato mistakenly posited forms that possessed these characteristics. While Aquinas uses the adverb *immobiliter* (immovably) for the third condition, we have translated 'immutable' instead, since Aquinas's point concerns change generally and not simply locomotion.

3 *ST* I, q. 86, a. 1 ad 3: 'Intelligibility is incompatible with the singular not as such, but as material, for nothing can be understood otherwise than immaterially.'

4 See *ST* I, q. 85, a. 3 corp.: 'Because sense has singular and individual things for its object, and the intellect has the universal for its object, it follows that our knowledge (*cognitio*) of the former comes before our knowledge of the latter.'

5 Aquinas draws the distinction between these two kinds of 'alteration' in *ST* I, q. 78, a. 3 corp.

6 Aquinas recognizes four internal sense powers: the 'common sense', imagination, estimation, and memory. In *ST* I, q. 78, a. 4 corp., he gives a brief overview of how these powers are distinguished and what each is supposed to do. We focus on the common sense and imagination for purposes of this chapter.

7 See *ST* I, q. 78, a. 4 ad 2, where Aquinas explains the difference between the proper senses (i.e. the five external senses) and the common sense power.

8 The term *phantasma* derives from *phantasia*, the Greek term for 'imagination'. The relation of the terms makes it clear that the phantasm is the product of the imagination. Aristotle explains the terms this way: 'If imagination (*phantasia*) is . . . the process by which we say that an image (*phantasma*) is presented to us, it is one of those faculties or states of mind by which we judge and are either right or wrong' (*De anima* book 3, chap. 3 (428a1–428a4), trans. W. S. Hett [Cambridge: Harvard University Press, 1957], 158–159).

9 See *ST* I, q. 84, aa. 2–5.

10 *ST* I, q. 84, a. 6 corp.; cf. *ST* I, q. 79, a. 3.

11 *ST* I, q. 85, a. 1 ad 4: 'Not only does the agent intellect illuminate phantasms, it does more: by its own power intelligible species are abstracted from phantasms.'

12 *ST* I, q. 85, a. 1 ad 1.

13 *ST* I, q. 85, a. 2 corp.

14 'Direct realism' here refers to the view that in perception one is directly aware of an object in the world, and thus outside the mind. By contrast,

'representationalism' holds that one cannot be aware of an object outside the mind without also being aware of an object inside the mind, which mediates between the mind and the extra-mental object. Aquinas is treated as a direct realist in N. Kretzmann, 'Philosophy of Mind', 138–42. For a representationalist interpretation of Aquinas on perception, see C. Panaccio, 'Aquinas on Intellectual Representation', in *Ancient and Medieval Theories of Intentionality*, ed. D. Perler (Leiden: Brill, 2001), 185–202. A nuanced account of Aquinas on this issue is found is R. Pasnau, *Theories of Cognition in the Later Middle Ages* (Cambridge: Cambridge University Press, 1997).

15 *ST* I, q. 84, a. 7 corp.
16 Ibid.
17 Aquinas quotes this passage from Aristotle's *De anima* book 3, chap. 7 (431a16) in *ST* I, q. 84, a. 7 sc.
18 *ST* I, q. 84, a. 7 corp. See also *ST* I, q. 85, a. 1.
19 Aristotle, *Categories*, chaps. 6–9. For a brief explanation of Aristotle's categories, see J. A. Oesterle, *Logic: The Art of Defining and Reasoning*, 2nd ed. (Englewood Cliffs, NJ: Prentice-Hall, 1963), 35–41.
20 Cf. the definition of 'science' in *The Concise Oxford Dictionary* as an 'organized body of the knowledge that has been accumulated on a subject'.
21 Aquinas, *Expositio libri Posteriorum* I, lectio 4. Trans. R. Berquist, *Commentary on Aristotle's Posterior Analytics* (Notre Dame, IN: Dumb Ox Books, 2007), 17–18. For a concise discussion of the Aristotelian concept of science as Aquinas understands it, see M. D. Jordan, *Ordering Wisdom: The Hierarchy of Philosophical Discourses in Aquinas* (Notre Dame, IN: University of Notre Dame Press, 1986), 75–83.
22 Aquinas, *In symbolum Apostolorum,* Proemium. This passage is discussed in R. Pasnau, *Thomas Aquinas on Human Nature: A Philosophical Study of Summa theologiae Ia 75–89* (Cambridge: Cambridge University Press, 2002), 166–168.
23 *ST* I, q. 85, a. 6 corp.: 'Every power, as such, is essentially directed to its proper object . . . Hence, as long as the power exists, its judgement concerning its own proper object does not fail. Now the proper object of the intellect is the quiddity in a thing. Hence, properly speaking, the intellect is not in error concerning this quiddity. . . .'
24 *ST* I, q. 85, a. 6 ad 1.
25 *ST* I, q. 88, a. 1 corp.: 'But in Aristotle's opinion, which experience corroborates, our intellect in its present state of life has a natural relationship to the natures of material things; and therefore it can only understand by turning to the phantasms. . . . Thus it clearly appears that immaterial substances, which do not fall under sense and imagination, cannot first and per se be known by us, according to the mode of knowledge of which we have experience.'
26 *ST* I, q. 88, a. 2 corp.
27 *Commentary on Aristotle's De anima* I.1, trans. R. Pasnau (New Haven, CT: Yale University Press, 1999), 11.
28 *ST* I, q. 87, a. 1 corp. and ad 1; ibid., q. 88, a. 2 ad 3.

29 *ST* I, q. 88, a. 2 ad 1: 'From material things we can rise to some kind of knowledge of immaterial things, but not to the perfect knowledge of them; for there is no proper and adequate proportion between material and immaterial things, and the likenesses drawn from material things for the understanding of immaterial things are very dissimilar to them.'

30 *ST* I, q. 88, a. 2 ad 4: 'Created immaterial substances are not in the same natural genus as material substances, for they do not agree in power or in matter; but they belong to the same logical genus, because even immaterial substances are in the predicament of substance, as their essence is distinct from their existence. . . . Hence through the likeness derived from material things we can know something positive concerning the angels, according to some common notion, though not according to the specific nature; whereas we cannot acquire any such knowledge at all about God.'

31 On the development of Aquinas's thought about the separated soul, see A. C. Pegis, 'The Separated Soul and its Nature in St. Thomas', in *St. Thomas Aquinas, 1274–1974: Commemorative Studies*, 2 vols. (Toronto: Pontifical Institute of Mediaeval Studies, 1974), 2: 131–158.

32 *ST* I, q. 3, a. 5 corp.

33 *ST* I, q. 12, a. 12 corp.

34 *ST* I, q. 12, a. 1 ad 4.

35 *ST* I, q. 12, a. 2 corp.

36 *ST* I, q. 12, a. 13 corp.

37 In relation to faith, Aquinas discusses gifts of understanding (*intellectus*) and knowledge (*scientia*) as examples of divine grace given to strengthen the mind's natural light; see *ST* II-II, qq. 8–9. For a discussion of how these gifts enable a greater understanding of truths of faith, see C. N. Still, 'Gifted Knowledge: An Exception to Thomistic Epistemology?', *The Thomist* 63 (1999): 173–190.

38 *ST* I, q. 12, a. 13 corp.

39 *ST* I, q. 12, a. 13 ad 3: 'Faith is a kind of cognition (*cognitio*), inasmuch as the intellect is determined by faith to some knowable object. But this determination to one object does not proceed from the vision of the believer, but from the vision of Him who is believed. Thus, as far as faith falls short of vision, it falls short of the nature that knowledge has when it is science (*scentia*); for science determines the intellect to one object by the vision and understanding of first principles.'

40 *ST* I, q. 12, a. 13 ad 1.

5 ETHICS

1 *ST* I-II, prologue.

2 *ST* I-II, q. 1, a. 1 corp.

3 *ST* I, q. 83, a. 1 corp.

4 Ibid.

5 Ibid.

6 *ST* I-II, q. 1, a. 2 corp.
7 On the view of final causality during the Scientific Revolution, see
M. J. Osler's *Divine Will and Mechanical Philosophy: Gassendi and
Descartes on Contingency and Necessity in the Created World* (Cambridge:
Cambridge University Press, 1994) and idem, 'Whose Ends? Teleology in
Early Modern Natural Philosophy,' *Osiris* 16 (2001): 151–168. For litera-
ture on Aristotle's theory of final causality, which immensely influenced
Aquinas's philosophy of nature, see M. R. Johnson, *Aristotle on Teleology*
(Oxford: Clarendon Press, 2005) and D. Sedley, 'Is Aristotle's Teleology
Anthropocentric?' *Phronesis* 36 (1991): 179–196. On natural philosophy
in the Middle Ages, see E. Grant, *God and Reason in the Middle Ages*
(Cambridge: Cambridge University Press, 2001) and E. D. Sylla, 'Creation
and Nature,' in *The Cambridge Companion to Medieval Philosophy*, ed.
A. S. McGrade (Cambridge: Cambridge University Press, 2003).
8 For a fuller discussion of this, see G. Braddock, 'Sartre on Atheism, Freedom, and Morality in *The Humanism of Existentialism*, in *Existentialist
Thinkers and Ethics*, ed. C. Daigle (Montreal and Kingston: McGill-
Queen's University Press, 2006), 91–106.
9 For Aquinas's famous 'Five Ways' or arguments for the existence of God,
see *ST* I, q. 2, a. 3 corp.
10 *ST* I-II, q. 1, a. 4 corp.
11 *ST* I-II, q. 5, a. 3 corp. See also, *ST* I-II, q. 2, a. 8 corp. and *ST* I-II, q. 5,
a. 1 corp.
12 *ST* I-II, q. 1, a. 7 corp. and *ST* I-II, q. 3, a. 4 corp.
13 *ST* I-II, q. 3, a. 1 corp.
14 *ST* I-II, q. 2, a. 1 corp.
15 *ST* I-II, q. 2, a. 2 corp.
16 On this, see *ST* I-II, q. 2, a. 4 corp.
17 *ST* I-II, q. 2, a. 8 corp.
18 *ST* I-II, q. 2, a. 1 ad 3
19 Ibid.
20 *ST* I-II, q. 5. a. 3 corp. See also *Summa contra gentiles* III, chap. 48:
'[A]ll men admit that felicity is a perfect good; otherwise, it could not
satisfy desire. Now, a perfect good is one which lacks any admixture of
evil, just as a perfectly white thing is completely unmixed with black. Of
course, it is not possible for man in the present state of life to be entirely
free from evils, not only from corporeal ones, such as hunger, thirst, heat
and cold, and other things of this kind, but also from evils of the soul.
For we can find no one who is not disturbed at times by unruly passions,
who does not at times overstep the mean in which virtue lies, either by
excess or defect, who also is not mistaken in certain matters, or who at
least is ignorant of things which he desires to know, or who also conceives with uncertain opinion things about which he would like to be
certain. Therefore, no person is happy in this life' (trans. Bourke, 164).
21 *ST* I, q. 9, a. 1 corp.
22 All of this seems somewhat counterintuitive. It suggests that we cannot
be happy in this life, which sounds bizarre. But Aquinas does actually
believe that a certain type of happiness can be achieved in the present life:

he just thinks that it is a diminished form. Aquinas therefore draws a distinction between 'perfect' happiness, which can only be achieved in the next life, and 'imperfect' happiness, which can be achieved in the here and now.

23 *ST* I-II, q. 3, a. 8 corp.
24 See P. S. Eardley, 'Conceptions of Happiness and Human Destiny in the Late Thirteenth Century.' *Vivarium* 44 (2006): 276–304.
25 *Summa contra gentiles* III, 26.
26 M.B. Crowe, *The Changing Profile of the Natural Law* (The Hague: Martinus Nijhoff, 1977), 1–18.
27 Ibid., 6–12.
28 Cicero, *De Re publica* III, 22 (Loeb Classical Library. Cambridge, MA: Harvard University Press, 1961), 210.
29 Cf. C. Nederman, 'Nature, Sin and the Origins of Society: The Ciceronian Tradition in Medieval Political Thought,' *Journal of the History of Ideas* 49 (1988): 3–26.
30 J. Coleman, *History of Political Thought: From the Middle Ages to the Renaissance* (Oxford: Blackwell, 2000), 106.
31 *ST* I-II, q. 90, a. 4 corp.
32 *ST* I-II, q. 90, a. 1 corp.
33 *ST* I-II, q. 90. a. 3 corp.
34 *ST* I-II, q. 92, a. 1 corp.
35 *ST* I-II, q. 90, a. 3 corp.
36 *ST* I-II, q. 90, a. 3 ad 1.
37 *ST* I-II, q. 90, a. 4 corp.
38 *ST* I-II, q. 96, a. 4 corp.: 'Unjust laws can be understood in a twofold way: first, by being contrary to the human good . . . either from the end, as when an authority imposes on his subjects onerous laws, which are conducive, not to the common good, but rather to his own cupidity or glory, or from the author, as when a man makes a law that goes beyond the power committed to him, or from the form, as when burdens are imposed unequally on the community, although with a view to the common good. The like are acts of violence rather than laws; because, as Augustine says . . . "a law that is unjust, seems to be no law at all." Therefore such laws do not bind in conscience . . .'
39 Such a condition seems reasonable enough with respect to human laws. But how is the natural law, or the eternal law, for that matter, 'promulgated'? In the case of human beings, God promulgates the law by implanting it in the minds of human beings. As Aquinas says in *ST* I-II, q. 90, a. 4 ad 1: 'The promulgation of the natural law is from the very fact that God placed it in the minds of human beings to be known naturally.'
40 *ST* I-II, q. 93, a. 5 corp.
41 *ST* I-II, q. 91, a. 2 corp.: '[N]ow, among others, the rational creature is subject to divine providence in the most excellent way, inasmuch as he participates in a share of providence, by being provident both for himself and for others.'

42 *ST* I-II, q. 10, a. 1 corp.: '[The] good in general, [is that] to which the will naturally tends, as does each power to its object. Again, this is the last end, which is related to appetible objects as the first principles of demonstrations to things intelligible.'

43 *ST* I-II, q. 91, a. 2 corp.: '[A]nd this participation of the eternal law in the rational creature is called the natural law . . . [which is] an imprint on us of the divine light.'

44 *De veritate* q. 16, a. 1 corp.: '[J]ust as there is a natural habit of the human soul through which it knows principles of the speculative sciences, which we call understanding of principles, so, too, there is in the soul a natural habit of first principles of action, which are the universal principles of natural law. This habit pertains to synderesis' (trans. J. V. McGlynn, 2: 304).

45 *ST* I-II, q. 94, a. 3 corp., Aquinas ultimately derives this principle from Aristotle's *Metaphysics,* book 4, chap. 3 (1005b19–1005b20).

46 *ST* I-II, q. 8, a. 1 corp.: 'It must be noted that, since every inclination follows a form, the natural appetite follows a form existing in the nature, while the sense appetite, as with the intellective or rational appetite, which is called the will, follows from an apprehended form. Therefore, just as the natural tends to good existing in a thing, so the animal or voluntary appetite tends to an apprehended good. Consequently, in order that the will tend to anything, it is necessary, not that it actually *be* good, but that it be *apprehended* as "good." Which is why the Philosopher says . . . that "the end is the good, or the apparent good."'

47 *ST* I-II, 1, q. 94, a. 2 corp.

48 Ibid.: 'In human beings there is first of all an inclination to the good in accordance with the nature which they have in common with all substances, insofar as every substance seeks the preservation of its own being according to its nature. And due to this inclination, whatever is a means of preserving human life, and of defending against its obstacles, belongs to the natural law.'

49 Ibid.: 'Secondly, there is in human beings an inclination to things that pertain to him more specifically, according to the nature which he has in common with other animals: and in virtue of this inclination, those things are said to belong to the natural law . . . such as sexual intercourse, education of offspring, etc.'

50 Ibid.: 'Thirdly, there is in human beings an inclination to the good according to the nature of reason, which is proper to them. Thus human beings have a natural inclination to know the truth about God, and to live in society: and in this respect, whatever pertains to this inclination belongs to the natural law; for instance, to avoid ignorance, to avoid offending those among whom one has to live, and other such things related to the above inclination.'

51 Aristotle, *Politics,* book 1, chap. 5 (1254b15–1255a3).

52 *ST* I-II, q. 94, a. 6 corp.

53 Ibid.

54 *ST* I-II, q. 95, a. 2 corp.: 'But note that something may be derived from the natural law in two ways: in one way, as a conclusion from premises,

in another way, by way of determination of certain generalities. The first mode is likened to that by which, in the sciences, demonstrated conclusions are drawn from the principles. But the second mode is likened to that whereby, in the arts, general forms are particularized with respect to details: thus the craftsman needs to determine the general form of a house to some particular shape. Some things are therefore derived from the general principles of the natural law by way of conclusions; for example, "one should not kill" may be derived as a conclusion from the principle that "one should not do harm to any person": while some are derived by way of determination; for example, the natural law states that the malefactor should be punished. However, that he should be punished in this way or that, is a determination of the natural law.'

55 *ST* I-II, q. 91, a. 4 corp.

56 Ibid.

57 *ST* I-II, q. 94, a. 3 corp.: 'We may speak of virtuous acts in two ways: in one way insofar as they are virtuous; in another way insofar as they are acts considered in their proper species. If then we speak of acts of virtue insofar as they are virtuous, in this way all virtuous acts belong to the natural law. For . . . [to] the natural law belongs everything to which a man is inclined according to his nature. Now each thing is inclined naturally to an operation that is suitable to it according to its form. Hence, fire is inclined to produce heat. Therefore, since the rational soul is the proper form of humanity, there is in every person a natural inclination to act according to reason: which is to act according to virtue. Considered in this way, then, all acts of virtue are prescribed by the law of nature, since each person's reason naturally dictates to him to act virtuously. But if we are referring to virtuous actions considered *in themselves*, that is, in their proper species, not all virtuous actions come from the natural law. This is because many things are done virtuously to which nature does not incline initially, but which, through the inquiry of reason, have been discovered by people to be conducive to well-living.'

58 For an excellent discussion of the ways in which Aquinas's virtue theory is inextricably tied to his theory of natural law, see Thomas Williams's introduction to Aquinas's *Disputed Questions on Virtues,* trans. E. M. Atkins (Cambridge: Cambridge University Press, 2005), ix–xxx.

59 *ST* I-II, q. 59, a. 1 corp.: '[T]he passions are not in themselves either good or bad. For good and bad in relation to humans is determined in reference to reason. Hence the passions, considered in themselves, can be good as well as evil insofar as they correspond to reason or are contrary to it.'

60 Aquinas, *On the Virtues in General,* a. 1.

61 J. Porter, 'Virtue Ethics,' in *The Cambridge Companion to Christian Ethics,* ed. R. Gill (Cambridge: Cambridge University Press, 2003), 102.

62 Cf. Aquinas, *ST* I-II, q. 55, a. 4 corp. and *On the Virtues in General,* a. 2; Peter Lombard, *Sentences* 2.27.1.1; Augustine, *On Free Will,* 2.19.

63 *ST* I-II, q. 62, a. 1 corp.

64 Aquinas, *On the Virtues in General,* a. 10 corp.

65 See Aristotle's *Nicomachean Ethics,* book 2.

66 *ST* I-II, q. 56, a. 3 corp. and *ST* I-II, q. 57, aa. 1–3.
67 Cf. Aristotle's *Nicomachean Ethics*, book 10.
68 Aquinas, *On the Virtues in General*, a. 2 corp.
69 *ST* II-II, q. 47, a. 1 corp.
70 *ST* I-II, q. 57, a. 4 corp.
71 *ST* I-II, q. 61, a. 3 corp.: '[J]ustice [is] the virtue which concerns due actions between equals . . .'
72 *ST* I-II, q. 60, a. 4 corp.
73 Aquinas, *On the Cardinal Virtues*, a. 1 corp.; *ST* I-II, q. 61, a. 3 corp.: '[T]emperance is [the virtue] that checks desire for the pleasures of touch . . .'
74 Ibid. a. 2 corp.: '[Just] as the moral virtues cannot exist without practical wisdom (i.e. prudence) . . . so practical wisdom cannot exist without the moral virtues: for practical wisdom is right reason in doing things' (trans. Atkins, 254).
75 Ibid., q. 5, ad 3.
76 Aquinas, *Commentary on the Ethics*, book 2, lecture 1: 'But we are perfected in these virtues by use, for when we act repeatedly according to reason, a modification is impressed in the appetite by the power of reason. This impression is nothing else but moral virtue'.
77 Ibid.: '[M]en become builders by building and harpists by playing the harp. Likewise men become just or temperate or courageous by doing just actions or temperate actions or courageous actions.'
78 Aquinas, *On the Virtues in General*, a. 1 corp.
79 *ST* II-II, q. 155, a. 1 corp.
80 *ST* I-II, q. 77, a. 2 corp. and *ST* II-II, q. 156, a. 1 corp., For some modern literature, see, for example, W. Charlton, *Weakness of Will* (Oxford: Basil Blackwell), 1988; D. Davidson, 'How is Weakness of the Will Possible?' in *Essays on Actions and Events* (Oxford: Clarendon Press, 1980), 21–42; J. Gosling, *Weakness of the Will* (London and New York: Routledge, 1990); and T. Hoffmann, ed., *Weakness of Will from Plato to the Present* (Washington, DC: The Catholic University of America Press, 2008).
81 *ST* I-II, q. 62, a. 1 corp.: 'Human beings are perfected through virtue by those actions in which they are ordered to happiness . . . However human happiness or felicity is twofold. . . . One is proportionate to human nature, to which namely human beings are able to arrive through the principles of their nature. The other is a happiness that exceeds human nature, and which man can only achieve by the power of God, by a certain participation in the divinity. . . . And because such happiness exceeds the capacity of human nature, man's natural principles, which allow him to act well according to his capacity, are not sufficient to direct human beings to this same happiness. Therefore it is necessary for human beings to receive from God some additional principles by which they may be directed to supernatural blessedness. . . . Such like principles are called 'theological virtues': first, because they have God for their object, insofar as they direct us properly to God; second, because they are infused in us by God alone; third, because these virtues are not made known to us except by divine revelation as contained in Holy Scripture.'

82 *ST* I-II, q. 63, a. 3 corp.: 'It should be said that effects must be proportionate to their causes and principles. However all virtues, intellectual as
well as moral, that are acquired by our actions, proceed from certain
natural principles pre-existing in us . . . In place of these natural principles, God confers on us the theological virtues through which we are
directed to a supernatural end.'

6 POLITICS

1 On the nature of women, see *ST* I, q. 92, a. 1 corp.: '[I]t was necessary for
woman to be made, as Scripture says, as a "helper" to man; not, however,
as a helper in other works, as some say, since man can be more efficiently
helped by another man in other works. Rather, [she was created to be] a
helper in the work of generation.' On heresy, see *ST* II-II, q. 11, a. 3 corp.:
'[W]ith regard to heretics two points must be observed: one, on their own
side; the other, on the side of the Church. On their own side there is the
sin, according to which they deserve not only to be cut off from the
Church by excommunication, but also to be cut off from the world by
death. For it is a much more serious matter to corrupt the faith which
strengthens the soul, than to forge money, which supports life in the here
and now. Therefore, if forgers of money and other malefactors are condemned to death by the secular authority, how much more justifiable is it
for heretics, as soon as they are convicted of heresy, to be not only excom-
municated but even executed.'
2 Cf. J. Dunbabin, 'The Reception and Interpretation of Aristotle's
Politics,' in the *Cambridge History of Later Medieval Philosophy*, ed.
N. Kretzmann et al. (Cambridge: Cambridge University Press, 1982),
724–737.
3 Aquinas, *De Regno*, book 1, chap. 4.
4 Ibid.
5 Aquinas, *Commentary on the Nicomachean Ethics*, book 1, lect. 1: '[M]an
receives help from the group of which he is a part, to have a perfect suf-
ficiency for life; namely, that man may not only live but live well, having
everything sufficient for living. And in this way, man is helped by the civic
group, of which he is a member, not only in regard to bodily needs . . . but
also in regard to right conduct, inasmuch as public authority restrains
with fear of punishment delinquent young men whom paternal admonition is not able to correct' (trans. Litzinger, 2).
6 See, for example, H. A. Deane, *The Political and Social Ideas of
St. Augustine* (New York: Columbia University Press, 1963), 39;
D. Bigongiari, 'The Political Ideas of St. Augustine,' in *Essays on Dante
and Medieval Culture* (Florence: L. S. Olschki, 1964), 94; and P. Weithman,
'Augustine and Aquinas on Original Sin and the Function of Political
Authority,' *Journal of the History of Philosophy* 30 (1992): 353–376.
7 Augustine, *City of God*, book 22, chap. 22: 'That the whole human race
has been condemned in its first origin, this life itself, if life it is to be
called, bears witness by the host of cruel ills with which it is filled. Is not

this proved by the profound and dreadful ignorance which produces all the errors that enfold the children of Adam, and from which no man can be delivered without toil, pain, and fear? Is it not proved by his love of so many vain and hurtful things, which produces gnawing cares, disquiet, griefs, fears, wild joys, quarrels, lawsuits, wars, treasons, angers, hatreds, deceit, flattery, fraud, theft, robbery, perfidy, pride, ambition, envy, murders, parricides, cruelty, ferocity, wickedness, luxury, insolence, impudence, shamelessness, fornications, adulteries, incests and the numberless uncleannesses and unnatural acts of both sexes, which it is shameful so much as to mention; sacrileges, heresies, blasphemies, perjuries, oppression of the innocent, calumnies, plots, falsehoods, false witnessings, unrighteous judgements, violent deeds, plunderings and whatever similar wickedness has found its way into the lives of men, though it cannot find its way into the conception of pure minds? These are indeed the crimes of wicked men, yet they spring from that root of error and misplaced love which is born with every son of Adam' (trans. Dods, 836), 1950.

8 Augustine, *City of God*, book 19, chap. 15.

9 D. Gauthier, *Rousseau: The Sentiment of Existence* (Cambridge: Cambridge University Press, 2006), 5–6. See also Jean-Jacques Rousseau, *A Discourse on Inequality*, trans. M. Cranston (Harmondsworth: Penguin, 1986).

10 Ibid.

11 *ST* I, q. 96, a. 4 corp.: 'First, man is naturally a social being, and so in the state of innocence he would have led a social life. But a social life cannot exist among a number of people unless it is under the direction of one person who looks after the common good. For many people seek many things, whereas one person attends only to one. Therefore the Philosopher says, at the beginning of the *Politics*, that wherever many things are directed to one, we shall always find one at the head directing them.'

12 *ST* I, q. 96, a. 4 corp.: 'Secondly, if one man surpassed another in knowledge and virtue, this would not have [happened] unless these gifts conduced to the benefit of others . . .'

13 For a contemporary defense of paternalism from a liberal perspective, see G. Dworkin, 'Paternalism,' in *Readings in the Philosophy of Law*, ed. K. Culver (Peterborough: Broadview Press, 1999), 342–356.

14 P. Sigmund, 'Law and Politics,' in *The Cambridge Companion to Aquinas*, ed. N. Kretzmann and E. Stump (Cambridge: Cambridge University Press, 1993).

15 *ST* I-II, q. 105, a. 1 corp.: 'Therefore, the best form of government is in a state or kingdom, in which one is given the power to preside over all; while under him are others having governing powers. Nonetheless, a government of this kind is shared by all, both because all are eligible to govern, and because the rules are chosen by all. For this is the best form of polity, being partly kingdom, since there is one at the head of all; partly aristocracy, in so far as a number of them are placed in authority; partly democracy, i.e. government by the people, in so far as the rulers can be chosen from the people, for the people have the right to choose their rulers.'

16 This was either Hugh II of Lusignan (1253–1267) or Hugh III of Antioch-Lusignan (1257–1284).
17 Sigmund, 'Law and Politics,' 221.
18 Aquinas, *De Regno*, book 1, chaps. 1–3.
19 *ST* II-II, q. 42, a. 2 corp.: 'Therefore it is clear that the unity to which sedition is opposed is the unity of law and the common utility. Hence it clearly follows that sedition is opposed to justice and the common good. Therefore by reason of its genus, it is a mortal sin, and its gravity will be all the greater according as the common good which it attacks surpasses the private good which is attacked by conflict.'
20 Ibid., ad 3.
21 *ST* I-II, q. 95, a. 1 corp.
22 Ibid.
23 Ibid.
24 J.S. Mill, *On Liberty*, chap. 1: 'Over himself, over his own body and mind, the individual is sovereign.'
25 Cf. C. Wolfe, *Natural Law Liberalism* (Cambridge: Cambridge University Press, 2006), 131–151. An equally famous defense of anti-perfectionist liberalism, although from a Kantian perspective, is John Rawls's monumentally influential *A Theory of Justice* (Cambridge, MA: Harvard University Press, 1971).
26 Mill, *On Liberty*, chap. 3.
27 Ibid., chap. 1: 'The only part of the conduct of anyone for which he is amenable to society is that which concerns others. In the part which merely concerns himself, his independence is, of right, absolute.'
28 Ibid.: '[T]he sole end for which mankind are warranted, individually or collectively, in interfering with the liberty of action of their number is self-protection. The only purpose for which power can be rightfully exercised over any member of a civilized community, against his will, is to prevent harm to others. His own good, wether physical or moral, is not sufficient warrant. He cannot rightfully be compelled to do so or forbear because it will make him happier, because, in the opinion of others, to do so would be wise or even right.'
29 This is not to deny that there are liberals who advocate perfectionism, only that Mill is not one of them. See J. Raz, *The Morality of Freedom* (Oxford: Clarendon Press, 1986).
30 See Wolfe, *Natural Law Liberalism*, 1.
31 For a fuller account of this, see Chapter 5.
32 On this, see T. M. Osborne, Jr., *Love of Self and Love of God in Thirteenth Century Ethics* (Notre Dame, IN: University of Notre Dame Press, 2005), 87–94; and M. S. Kempshall, *The Common Good in Late Medieval Political Thought* (Oxford: Clarendon Press, 1999).
33 Aquinas, *Commentary on Aristotle's Politics*, book 1, lect. 1, n. 11.
34 G. Froelich, 'The Equivocal Status of *Bonum Commune*,' *The New Scholasticism* 63 (1989): 38.
35 I. Eschmann, 'In Defense of Jacques Maritain,' *The Modern Schoolman* 22 (1945): 198, n. 24.

36 W. Kymlicka, *Contemporary Political Philosophy: An Introduction* (Oxford: Clarendon Press, 1990), 206.
37 Aquinas, *On the Virtues in General*, a. 9 corp.
38 Aquinas, *Disputed Questions on Charity*, a. 2 corp.
39 *ST* I-II, q. 5, a. 7 corp.
40 *ST* I-II,, q. 66, a. 4 corp.: 'A virtue according to its own species can be said to be greater or less, either without qualification (*simpliciter*) or in a relative sense (*secundum quid*). A virtue is said to be greater without qualification, insofar as a greater rational good of reason manifests itself . . . In this way justice is the most excellent of all the moral virtues, being closest to reason. This is clear by considering both its subject and its object: on the side of its subject, because it is in the will as its subject and the will is the rational appetite. On the side of its object or matter, however, because it concerns activities by which man is ordered not only to himself, but also to another. Hence "justice is the most excellent of the virtues."'
41 Ibid., II-II, q. 58, a. 4 corp.
42 Ibid., q. 58, a. 1 corp.
43 Ibid., a. 5 corp.: 'Justice . . . orders man in his relations with other men. This may occur in two ways: in one way as regards his relations with individuals, secondly with respect to his relations with others in general, inasmuch as he who serves a community, serves all those who are included in that community . . . Now, it is clear that all who are included in a community, stand in relation to that community as parts to a whole; while a part, as such, belongs to a whole, so that whatever is the good of a part can be ordered to the good of the whole. Consequently the good of any virtue, whether such virtue orders a man in relation to himself, or in relation to other individuals, is referable to the common good, to which justice orders. Therefore all acts of virtue can pertain to justice, insofar as it orders man to the common good. It is in this way that justice is called a general virtue. And since it pertains to the law to direct to the common good, . . . it follows that the justice which is in this way called 'general,' is called 'legal justice,' because by it man is in harmony with the law that directs the acts of all the virtues to the common good.'
44 Quoted in P. Longman, 'The Return of Patriarchy,' *Foreign Policy* 153 (2006): 62. Cf. also S. B. Hrdy, *Mother Nature: Maternal Instincts and How They Shape the Human Species* (New York: Ballantine, 1999).
45 Ibid., 63.
46 *ST* I-II, q. 96, a. 2 ad 2.
47 Ibid., corp.
48 Aquinas, *Disputed Question on Charity*, a. 2 corp.
49 Ibid., a. 3 corp.
50 Given the modern Catholic church's strict stance on abortion, it might be surprising to find that Aquinas has a much more nuanced attitude towards abortion. On this, see R. Pasnau, *Thomas Aquinas on Human Nature* (Cambridge: Cambridge University Press, 2002), 105–120.

51 For a sketch of the history of just war theory, see B. Orend, *The Morality of War* (Peterborough, ON: Broadview Press, 2006), 9–27. See also J. Johnson, 'The Idea of Defense in Historical and Contemporary Thinking about Just War,' *Journal of Religious Ethics* 36 (2008): 543–556; and idem, *The Just War Tradition and the Restraint of War* (Princeton: Princeton University Press, 1981).

52 Orend, *The Morality of War*, 2.

53 Ibid.

54 Thucydides, *On Justice, Power and Human Nature: Selections from The History of the Peloponnesian War*, ed. and trans. P. Woodruff (Indianapolis: Hackett Publishing Company, 1993), 106.

55 Orend, *The Morality of War*, 244–246.

56 M. Walzer, *Just and Unjust Wars* (New York: Basic Books, 1977), 330–335.

57 Orend, *The Morality of War*, 244–250.

58 Quoted in ibid., 244.

59 *ST* II-II, q. 40, a. 1 corp.: 'In order for a war to be just, three things are required. First, the authority of the sovereign by whose command the war is to be fought. For it is not the business of a private individual to declare war, because he can seek for redress of his rights from the court of his superior. Similarly it is not his business to mobilize the people, which it is necessary to do in wartime. And as the care of the common good is committed to those who are in authority, it is their business to watch over the common good of the city, kingdom, or province subject to them. And just as it is licit for them to have recourse to the sword in defending that common good against internal threats, when they punish malefactors . . . so too, it is their business to have recourse to war in defending the common good against external enemies.'

60 Ibid.

61 See Orend, *The Morality of War*, 31–46.

62 *ST* II-II, q. 40, a. 1 corp.

63 Ibid., ad 2: '. . . it is necessary occasionally for a man to act otherwise for the common good, or for the good of those with whom he is fighting. Hence Augustine says: "Those whom we have to punish with a kindly severity, it is necessary to handle in many ways against their will. For when we are stripping a man of the lawlessness of sin, it is good for him to be conquered, since nothing is more hopeless than the happiness of sinners, from which condition arises a guilty impunity, and an evil will, like an internal enemy."'

64 Ibid., corp.

65 Ibid., corp.: 'Thirdly, it is required that the belligerents should have a moral intention, so that they intend the furtherance of good, or the avoidance of evil. Hence Augustine says . . . "True religion looks upon as peaceful those wars that are waged not for cupidity or cruelty, but for securing peace, for punishing the wicked, and for raising up the good." For it can happen that a war is declared by a legitimate authority, and for a just cause, and yet become illicit through a wrong intention.

Hence Augustine says . . . "The cupidity for inflicting harm, the cruelty of vengeance, a restless and relentless spirit, the fever of rebellion, the lust for power, and similar things, are all rightly condemned in war."'

66 *ST* II-II, q. 64, a. 7 corp. '[N]othing prevents one action from having two effects, of which only one is intended, but the other is beyond the intention. Now moral acts receive their species according to what is intended, and not according to what is beyond the intention, since this is accidental . . . Therefore the act of self-defense may have two effects, one is the saving of one's life, the other is the killing of the aggressor. Therefore since one's intention was to save one's own life, this action is not unlawful, given that it is natural to everything to preserve itself as far as possible. However, an act may be rendered unlawful even though proceeding from a good intention if it is not proportioned to the end. Therefore if a person, in self-defense, uses more than violence than is necessary, it will be illicit, whereas if he defends himself with moderate force his defense will be licit . . . Nor is it required for salvation that someone omit the act of moderate self-defense to avoid killing the other person, since one is obligated to take more care of one's own life than of another's. But as it is illicit to take a man's life, except for the public authority acting for the common good . . . it is not licit for a man to intend killing a man in self-defense, except for those who have public authority, who while intending to kill a man in self-defense, refer this to the public good, e.g., a soldier fighting against an enemy . . .'

BIBLIOGRAPHY

PRIMARY WORKS IN LATIN

Although there are several Latin editions of the collected works of Aquinas, the most authoritative version is the so-called Leonine edition:

Sancti Thomae Aquinatis Doctoris Angelici. Opera Omnia. Iussu Leonis XIII. Rome: Vatican Polyglot Press, 1882–.

MAJOR WORKS IN ENGLISH TRANSLATION

Disputed Questions on Truth. Trans. R. Mulligan, J. V. McGlynn, and R. Schmidt. 3 vols. Chicago: Henry Regnery Co., 1952–1954.
Disputed Questions on the Virtues. Trans. E. M. Atkins. Cambridge: Cambridge University Press, 2005.
On Evil. Trans. R. Regan. New York and Oxford: Oxford University Press, 2001.
On the Power of God. Trans. English Dominican Fathers. London: Burns, Oates, and Washbourne, 1932–1934.
On Spiritual Creatures. Trans. M. C. Fitzpatrick. Milwaukee: Marquette University Press, 1951.
Questions on the Soul. Trans. J. H. Robb. Milwaukee: Marquette University Press, 1984.
Quodlibetal Questions I and II. Trans. S. Edwards. Toronto: Pontifical Institute of Mediaeval Studies, 1983.
Summa contra gentiles. Trans. English Dominican Fathers. London: Burns, Oates, and Washbourne, 1934.
Summa Theologiae. Trans. English Dominican Fathers. London: Burns, Oates, and Washburne, 1912–1936; New York: Benziger, 1947–1948; New York: Christian Classics, 1981.
The Treatise on Human Nature: Summa theologiae 1a 75–89. Trans. R. Pasnau. Indianapolis: Hackett, 2002.

MINOR WORKS IN ENGLISH TRANSLATION

An Aquinas Reader. Ed. M. Clark. New York: Image Books, 1972.
Aquinas against the Averroists: On there Being only One Intellect. Trans. R. McInerny. West Lafayette, IN: Purdue University Press, 1993.

Treatise on Separate Substances. Trans. F. J. Lescoe. West Hartford, CT.: St Joseph College, 1959.

On Being and Essence. Trans. A. Maurer. 2nd edition. Toronto: Pontifical Institute of Mediaeval Studies, 1968.

De principiis naturae ad fratrem Sylvestrum. Trans. R. Kocourek. St. Paul: North Central, 1948.

On the Eternity of the World. Trans. C. Vollert. Milwaukee: Marquette University Press, 1964.

The Opusculum on Lots of St. Thomas. Trans. P. B. Carey. Dover, MA: Dominican House of Philosophy, 1963.

On Kingship. Trans. G. B. Phelan. Toronto: Pontifical Institute of Mediaeval Studies, 1946.

The Compendium of Theology. Trans. C. Vollert. St. Louis: Herder, 1947.

COMMENTARIES IN ENGLISH TRANSLATION

A Commentary on Aristotle's De anima. Trans. R. Pasnau. New Haven: Yale University Press, 1999.

Aristotle on Interpretation: Commentary by St. Thomas and Cajetan. Trans. J. T. Oesterle. Milwaukee: Marquette University Press, 1962.

Aristotle's De Anima with the Commentary of St. Thomas Aquinas. Trans. K. Foster and S. Humphries. New Haven: Yale University Press, 1951.

Commentary on Aristotle's Physics. Trans. R. J. Blackwell et al. New Haven: Yale University Press, 1963.

Commentary on Aristotle's 'Politics'. Trans. E. Fortin and P. O'Neill. In *Medieval Political Philosophy: A Sourcebook*. Ed. R. Lerner. New York: Free Press, 1963.

Commentary on Aristotle's Posterior Analytics. Trans. R. Berquist. Notre Dame, IN: Dumb Ox Books, 2007.

Commentary on the Metaphysics of Aristotle. Trans. J. P. Rowan. Chicago: Henry Regnery, 1962.

Commentary on the Nicomachean Ethics. Trans. C. I. Litzinger. Chicago: Henry Regnery, 1964.

Commentary on St. John. Trans. J. A. Weisheipl with F. R. Larcher, Vol. 1. Albany, NY: Magi Books, 1980.

Commentary on St. Paul's Epistle to the Ephesians. Trans. M. L. Lamb. Albany, NY: Magi Books, 1966.

Commentary on St. Paul's Epistle to the Galatians. Trans. F. R. Larcher. Albany, NY: Magi Books, 1966.

Commentary on St. Paul's Epistle to the Philippians. Trans. F. R. Larcher. Albany, NY: Magi Books, 1968.

Commentary on St. Paul's Epistle to the Thessalonians. Trans. M. Duffy. Albany, NY: Magi Books, 1968.

On Love and Charity: Readings from the 'Commentary on the Sentences of Peter Lombard'. Trans. P. A. Kwasniewski, T. Bolin, and J. Bolin. Washington, DC: Catholic University of America Press, 2008.

The Division and Methods of the Sciences, Questions V-VI of the Commentary on Boethius' De Trinitate. Trans. A. A. Maurer. 4th edition. Toronto: Pontifical Institute of Mediaeval Studies, 1986.

Faith, Reason, and Theology, Questions I-IV of his Commentary on the De Trinitate of Boethius. Trans. A. A. Maurer. Toronto: Pontifical Institute of Mediaeval Studies, 1987.

The Literal Exposition of Job: A Scriptural Commentary concerning Providence. Trans. A. Damico. Atlanta: Scholars Press, 1989.

SOURCES ON THE LIFE OF AQUINAS

Foster, K., ed. *The Life of Thomas Aquinas.* London: Longmans, 1959.

Torrell, J. -P. *Saint Thomas Aquinas:* Vol. 1, *The Person and His Work.* Trans. Robert Royal. Washington: Catholic University of America Press, 1996.

Weisheipl, J. A. *Friar Thomas D'Aquino: His Life, Thought, and Work.* Washington: Catholic University of America Press, 1984/original; 1974. paperback.

PRIMARY WORKS BY AUTHORS OTHER THAN AQUINAS

Anselm. *Basic Writings.* Trans. T. Williams. Indianapolis: Hackett, 2007.

Aristotle. *The Complete Works of Aristotle.* Ed. J. Barnes. 2 vols. Princeton: Princeton University Press, 1984.

—*On the Soul, Parva Naturalia, On Breath.* Trans. W. S. Hett. Reprint edition. Cambridge, MA: Harvard University Press, 2000.

Augustine. *The City of God.* Trans. M. Dods. New York: Modern Library, 1950.

—*On Free Choice of the Will.* Trans. A. S. Benjamin and L. H. Hackstaff. New York: Macmillan, 1964.

Cicero. *De Re publica.* Trans. C. W. Keyes. Loeb Classical Library. Cambridge, MA: Harvard University Press, 1961.

Darwin, C. *Origin of Species by Means of Natural Selection.* New York: Modern Library, 1993.

Descartes, R. *Meditations on First Philosophy.* 3rd edition. Trans. D. A. Cress. Indianapolis: Hackett, 1993.

Mill, J. S. *On Liberty.* Ed. E. Alexander. Peterborough, ON: Broadview Press, 1999.

Rousseau, J. -J. *A Discourse on Inequality.* Trans. M. Cranston. Harmondsworth: Penguin, 1986.

Thucydides. *On Justice, Power and Human Nature: Selections from The History of the Peloponnesian War.* Ed. and trans. P. Woodruff. Indianapolis: Hackett Publishing Company, 1993.

SECONDARY LITERATURE

Aertsen, J. *Nature and Creature: Thomas Aquinas' Way of Thought.* Leiden: E. J. Brill, 1988.

—'The Convertibility of Being and Good in St. Thomas Aquinas'. *The New Scholasticism* 59 (1985): 449–470.

—*Medieval Philosophy and the Transcendentals: The Case of Thomas Aquinas*. Leiden: E. J. Brill, 1996.

Anscombe, G. E. M. and Geach, P. T. *Three Philosophers*. Ithaca: Cornell University Press, 1961.

Armstrong, R. A. *Primary and Secondary Precepts in Thomistic Natural Law Teaching*. The Hague: Nijhoff, 1966.

Bigongiari, D. 'The Political Ideas of St. Augustine'. In *Essays on Dante and Medieval Culture*. Florence: L. S. Olschki, 1964.

Black, A. *Political Thought in Europe: 1250–1450*. Cambridge: Cambridge University Press, 1992.

Bobik, J. *Aquinas on Matter and Form and the Elements*. Notre Dame: University of Notre Dame Press, 1998.

Bonnette, D. *Aquinas' Proofs for God's Existence*. The Hague: Nijhoff, 1972.

Bowlin, J. *Contingency and Fortune in Aquinas's Ethics*. Cambridge: Cambridge University Press, 1999.

Boyle, L. 'The *De regno* and the Two Powers'. In *Essays in Honour of Anton Charles Pegis*. Ed. R. J. O'Donnell, 237–247. Toronto: Pontifical Institute of Mediaeval Studies, 1974.

Braddock, G. 'Sartre on Atheism, Freedom, and Morality. In *The Humanism of Existentialism*'. In *Existentialist Thinkers and Ethics*. Ed. C. Daigle, 91–106. Montreal and Kingston: McGill-Queen's University Press, 2006.

Bradley, D. J. M. *Aquinas on the Twofold Human Good*. Washington, DC: Catholic University of America Press, 1997.

Brett, A. S. 'Political Philosophy'. In *The Cambridge Companion to Medieval Philosophy*. Ed. A. S. McGrade, 276–299. Cambridge: Cambridge University Press, 2003.

Burrell, D. *Aquinas: God and Action*. Notre Dame: University of Notre Dame Press, 1985.

—*Knowing the Unknowable God: Ibn Sina, Maimondies, Aquinas*. Notre Dame: University of Notre Dame Press, 1986.

Canning, J. *A History of Medieval Political Thought: 300–1450*. London and New York: Routledge, 1996.

Carroll, T. 'The Traditions of Fideism'. *Religious Studies* 44 (2008): 1–22.

Cessario, R. *A Short History of Thomism*. Washington, DC: Catholic University of America Press, 2005.

Charlton, W. *Weakness of Will*. Oxford: Basil Blackwell, 1988.

Chenu, M. -D. *Toward Understanding St. Thomas*. Chicago: Henry Regnery, 1964.

Clark, W. N. *Explorations in Metaphysics: Being – God – Person*. Notre Dame, IN: University of Notre Dame Press, 1994.

—*The One and the Many: A Contemporary Thomistic Metaphysics*. Notre Dame, IN: University of Notre Dame Press, 2001.

Coleman, J. *A History of Political Thought: From the Middle Ages to the Renaissance*. Oxford: Blackwell, 2000.

Copleston, F. C. *Aquinas*. Harmondsworth: Penguin, 1955.

Cross, R. *Duns Scotus*. Oxford: Oxford University Press, 1999.

Crowe, M. B. *The Changing Profile of the Natural Law*. The Hague: Nijhoff, 1977.

Dales, R. *Medieval Discussion of the Eternity of the World*. Leiden and Boston: Brill, 1990.

Davidson, D. 'How is Weakness of the Will Possible?' In *Essays on Actions and Events, 21–42*. Oxford: Clarendon Press, 1980.

Davies, B. *The Thought of Thomas Aquinas*. Oxford: Clarendon Press, 1992.

Dawkins, R. *The God Delusion*. Boston: Houghton Mifflin, 2006.

Deane, H. A. *The Political and Social Ideas of St. Augustine*. New York: Columbia University Press, 1963.

Dewan, L. 'St. Thomas on Analogy: The Logician and the Metaphysician'. In *Laudemus viros gloriosus: Essays in Honour of Armand Maurer, CSB*. Ed. R. E. Houser, 132–145. Notre Dame, IN: University of Notre Dame Press, 2007.

Donagan, A. 'Thomas Aquinas on Human Action'. In *The Cambridge History of Later Medieval Philosophy*. Ed. N. Kretzmann et al., 642–654. Cambridge: Cambridge University Press, 1982.

Dougherty, M. V. 'Thomas Aquinas and Divine Command Theory'. *Proceedings of the American Catholic Philosophical Association* 76 (2002): 153–164.

—'Aquinas and the Self-Evidence of the Articles of Faith'. *The Heythrop Journal* 46.2 (2005): 167–180.

—'Thomas Aquinas on the Manifold Senses of Self-Evidence'. *The Review of Metaphysics* 59.3 (2006): 601–630.

Dunbabin, J. 'The Reception and Interpretation of Aristotle's *Politics*'. In *The Cambridge History of Later Medieval Philosophy*. Ed. N. Kretzmann et al., 724–737. Cambridge: Cambridge University Press, 1982.

Dworkin, G. 'Paternalism'. In *Readings in the Philosophy of Law*. Ed. K. Culver, 342–356. Peterborough: Broadview Press, 1999.

Eardley, P. S. 'Thomas Aquinas and Giles of Rome on the Will'. *Review of Metaphysics* 56 (2003): 835–862.

—'Conceptions of Happiness and Human Destiny in the Late Thirteenth Century'. *Vivarium* 44 (2006): 276–304.

—'The Foundations of Freedom in Later Medieval Philosophy: Giles of Rome and His Contemporaries'. *Journal of the History of Philosophy* 44 (2006): 353–376.

Eco, U. *Art and Beauty in the Middle Ages*. New Haven: Yale University Press, 1986.

Elders, L. *The Philosophical Theology of St. Thomas Aquinas*. Leiden: E. J. Brill, 1990.

Eschmann, I. 'In Defense of Jacques Maritain'. *The Modern Schoolman* 22 (1945): 183–208.

—*The Ethics of Saint Thomas Aquinas*. Toronto: Pontifical Institute of Mediaeval Studies, 1997.

Finnis, J. *Aquinas: Moral, Legal, and Political Theory*. New York: Oxford University Press, 1998.

Flannery, K. L. *Acts Amid Precepts: The Aristotelian Logical Structure of Thomas Aquinas's Moral Theory*. Washington, DC: Catholic University of America Press, 2001.

Fox, R. *Time and Eternity in Mid-Thirteenth-Century Thought*. Oxford: Oxford University Press, 2006.

Froelich, G. 'The Equivocal Status of *Bonum Commune*'. *The New Scholasticism* 63 (1989): 38–57.

Gauthier, D. *Rousseau: The Sentiment of Existence*. Cambridge: Cambridge University Press, 2006.

Geach, P. *God and the Soul*. London: Routledge and Kegan Paul, 1969.

Gilson, E. *The Christian Philosophy of St. Thomas Aquinas*. Trans. L. K. Shook. New York: Random House, 1956; Notre Dame, IN: University of Notre Dame Press, 1994.

Goris, H. *Free Creatures of an Eternal God: Thomas Aquinas on God's Infallible Foreknowledge and Irresistible Will*. Leuven: Peeters, 1996.

Gosling, J. *Weakness of the Will*. London and New York: Routledge, 1990.

Goyette, J., Latkovic, M. and Meyers, R., eds. *St. Thomas Aquinas and the Natural Law Tradition: Contemporary Perspectives*. Washington, DC: Catholic University of America Press, 2004.

Grant, E. *God and Reason in the Middle Ages*. Cambridge: Cambridge University Press, 2001.

Grisez, G. 'The First Principles of Practical Reason: A Commentary on *ST* q. 94, a. 2'. *Natural Law Forum* 10 (1965): 168–201.

Haldane, J. 'Aquinas on Sense Perception'. *The Philosophical Review* 92 (1983): 233–239.

Hall, P. M. *Narrative and the Natural Law: An Interpretation of Thomistic Ethics*. Notre Dame, IN: University of Notre Dame Press, 1994.

Hankey, W. *God in Himself: Aquinas' Doctrine of God as Expounded in the 'Summa Theologiae'*. Oxford: Oxford University Press, 1987.

Harak, G. *Virtuous Passions: The Formation of Christian Character*. NY: Paulist Press, 1993.

Harrison, P. *The Fall of Man and the Foundations of Science*. Cambridge: Cambridge University Press, 2007.

Hause, J. 'Thomas Aquinas and the Voluntarists'. *Medieval Philosophy and Theology* 6.2 (1997): 167–182.

Hibbs, T. *Dialectic and Narrative in Aquinas: An Interpretation of the 'Summa Contra Gentiles'*. Notre Dame, IN: University of Notre Dame Press, 1995.

—*Aquinas, Ethics, and Philosophy of Religion: Metaphysics and Practice*. Bloomington: Indiana University Press, 2007.

Hoffman, T. 'Aquinas on the Moral Progress of the Weak Willed'. In *Das Problem der Willensschwächen mittlelalterlichen Philosophie/The Problem of Weakness of Will in Medieval Philosophy*. Ed. T. Hoffman et al. 221–247. Leuven: Peeters, 2006.

—'Aquinas and Intellectual Determinism: The Test Case of Angelic Sin'. *Archiv für Geschichte der Philosophie* 89 (2007): 122–156.

—'Albert the Great and Thomas Aquinas on Magnanimity'. In *Virtue Ethics in the Middle Ages: Commentaries on Aristotle's Ethics (1200–1500).* Ed. I. Bejczy, 101–29. Leiden: E. J. Brill, 2008.

Hoffman, T., ed. *Weakness of Will from Plato to the Present.* Washington, DC: The Catholic University of America Press, 2008.

Hrdy, S. B. *Mother Nature: Maternal Instincts and How They Shape the Human Species.* New York: Ballantine, 1999.

Hughes, C. *On a Complex Theory of a Simple God: An Investigation in Aquinas' Philosophical Theology.* Ithaca: Cornell University Press, 1990.

Irwin, T. *The Development of Ethics. A Historical and Critical Study.* Vol. 1, *From Socrates to the Reformation.* Oxford: Oxford University Press, 2007.

Jenkins, J. *Knowledge and Faith in Thomas Aquinas.* Cambridge and New York: Cambridge University Press, 1997.

Johnson, J. 'The Idea of Defense in Historical and Contemporary Thinking about Just War'. *Journal of Religious Ethics* 36 (2008): 543–556.

—*The Just War Tradition and the Restraint of War.* Princeton: Princeton University Press, 1981.

Johnson, M. F. 'Immateriality and the Domain of Thomistic Natural Philosophy'. *Modern Schoolman* 67 (1990): 285–304.

—'The Sapiential Character of the First Article of the *Summa theologiae*'. In *Philosophy and the God of Abraham: Essays in Memory of James A. Weisheipl, OP.* Ed. R. J. Long, 85–98. Toronto: Pontifical Institute of Mediaeval Studies, 1991.

—'Why Five Ways?' *American Catholic Philosophical Quarterly* 65 (1991): 107–121.

—'Aquinas's Changing Evaluation of Plato on Creation'. *American Catholic Philosophical Quarterly* 66 (1992): 39–46.

—'St Thomas and the 'Law of Sin'. *Recherches de théologie et philosophie médiévale* 67 (2000): 90–106.

Johnson, M. R. *Aristotle on Teleology.* Oxford: Clarendon Press, 2005.

Jordan, M. D. *Ordering Wisdom: The Hierarchy of Philosophical Discourses in Aquinas.* Notre Dame, IN: University of Notre Dame Press, 1986.

—'Theology and Philosophy'. In *The Cambridge Companion to Aquinas.* Ed. N. Kretzmann and E. Stump, 232–251. Cambridge: Cambridge University Press, 1993.

—'The Alleged Aristotelianism of Thomas Aquinas'. In *The Gilson Lectures on Thomas Aquinas*, 73–106. Toronto: Pontifical Institute of Mediaeval Studies, 2008.

Kempshall, M. S. *The Common Good in Late Medieval Political Thought.* Oxford: Clarendon Press, 1999.

Kenny, A. *Aquinas.* Oxford: Oxford University Press, 1980.

—*The Five Ways: St. Thomas Aquinas' Proofs of God's Existence.* Notre Dame, IN: University of Notre Dame Press, 1980.

—*Aquinas on Mind.* London: Routledge, 1993.

—*Aquinas on Being.* Oxford: Clarendon Press, 2002.

Kent, B. 'Transitory Vice: Thomas Aquinas on Incontinence'. *Journal of the History of Philosophy* 27 (1989): 199–223.

—*Virtues of the Will: The Transformation of Ethics in the Late Thirteenth Century.* Washington, DC: Catholic University of America Press, 1995.

Kerr, F. *After Aquinas: Versions of Thomism.* Oxford: Blackwell, 2002.

Keys, M. M. *Aquinas, Aristotle, and the Promise of the Common Good.* Cambridge: Cambridge University Press, 2006.

Klima, G. 'The Semantic Principles Underlying Saint Thomas Aquinas's Metaphysics of Being'. *Medieval Philosophy and Theology* 5 (1996): 87–141.

Knuuttila, S. *Emotions in Ancient and Medieval Philosophy.* Oxford: Clarendon Press, 2004.

Kretzmann, N. 'Philosophy of Mind'. In *The Cambridge Companion to Aquinas.* Ed. N. Kretzmann and E. Stump, 128–159. Cambridge: Cambridge University Press, 1993.

—*The Metaphysics of Theism.* Oxford: Clarendon Press, 1997.

—*The Metaphysics of Creation.* Oxford: Clarendon Press, 1999.

Kretzmann, N. and E, Stump, eds. *The Cambridge Companion to Aquinas.* Cambridge: Cambridge University Press, 1993.

Kymlicka, W. *Contemporary Political Philosophy: An Introduction.* Oxford: Clarendon Press, 1990.

Levering, M. *Scripture and Metaphysics: Aquinas and the Renewal of Trinitarian Theology.* Oxford: Blackwell, 2004.

Lewis, C. S. *The Discarded Image.* Cambridge: Cambridge University Press, 1964.

Lisska, A. J. *Aquinas' Theory of Natural Law: An Analytical Reconstruction.* New York: Oxford University Press, 1996.

Lonergan, B. *Grace and Freedom: Operative Grace in the Thought of St. Thomas Aquinas.* New York: Herder and Herder, 1971.

Longman, P. 'The Return of Patriarchy'. *Foreign Policy* 153 (2006): 56–65.

MacDonald, S., ed. 'Aquinas's Parasitic Cosmological Argument'. *Medieval Philosophy and Theology* 1 (1991): 134–173.

—'Aquinas's Libertarian Account of Free Choice'. *Revue Internationale de Philosophie* 52 (1998): 309–328.

—'Aquinas's Ultimate Ends: A Reply to Grisez'. *American Journal of Jurisprudence* 46 (2001): 37–49.

MacDonald, S. ed. *Being and Goodness: The Concept of the Good in Metaphysics and Philosophical Theology.* Ithaca: Cornell University Press, 1991.

—'Ultimate Ends in Practical Reasoning: Aquinas's Aristotelian Moral Psychology and Anscombe's Fallacy'. *The Philosophical Review* 100 (1991): 31–66

MacIntyre, A. *Whose Justice? Which Rationality?* London: Duckworth, 1988.

—*Three Rival Versions of Moral Inquiry.* Notre Dame, IN: University of Notre Dame Press, 1991.

Mackie, J. L. *The Miracle of Theism: Arguments for and Against the Existence of God.* Oxford: Clarendon Press, 1982.

Makin, S. 'Aquinas, Natural Tendencies and Natural Kinds'. *The New Scholasticism* 63 (1989): 253–274.

Malloy, M. *Civil Authority in Medieval Philosophy: Lombard, Aquinas, and Bonaventure*. Lanham: University Press of America, 1985.

Martin, C. J. F. *Thomas Aquinas: God and Explanations*. Edinburgh: Edinburgh University Press, 1997.

Martin, C. *The Philosophy of Thomas Aquinas*. London: Routledge, 1988.

Maurer, A. A. *Being and Knowing: Studies in Thomas Aquinas and Later Medieval Philosophers*. Toronto: Pontifical Institute of Mediaeval Studies, 1990.

McEvoy, J. and M. Dunne, eds. *Thomas Aquinas: Approaches to Truth*. Dublin: Four Courts Press, 2002.

McInerny, R. *Being and Predication*. Washington, DC: Catholic University of America Press, 1986.

—*Aquinas on Human Action: A Theory of Practice*. Washington, DC: Catholic University of America Press, 1992.

—*Aquinas and Analogy*. Washington, DC: Catholic University of America Press, 1996.

—*The Logic of Analogy: An Interpretation of St. Thomas*. Springer, 2001.

Milbank, J. and C. Pickstock. *Truth in Aquinas*. London and New York: Routledge, 2000.

Murphy, C. 'Aquinas on our Responsibility for Our Emotions'. *Medieval Philosophy and Theology* 8 (1999): 163–205.

Murphy, M. C. 'The Natural Law Tradition in Ethics,' in *The Stanford Encyclopedia of Philosophy* (http://plato.stanford.edu/entries/natural-law-ethics).

—*Natural Law and Practical Rationality*. Cambridge: Cambridge University Press, 2001.

Nederman, C. 'Nature, Sin and the Origins of Society: The Ciceronian Tradition in Medieval Political Thought'. *Journal of the History of Ideas* 49 (1988): 3–26.

Nelson, D. M. *The Priority of Prudence: Virtue and the Natural Law in Thomas Aquinas and the Implications for Modern Ethics*. University Park: Pennsylvania State University Press, 1992.

Novak, J. 'Aquinas and the Incorruptibility of the Soul'. *History of Philosophy Quarterly* 4 (1987): 405–421.

O'Callaghan, J. P. *Thomist Realism and the Linguistic Turn*. Notre Dame, IN: University of Notre Dame Press, 2003.

Oesterle, J. A. *Logic: The Art of Defining and Reasoning*. 2nd edition. Englewood Cliffs, NJ: Prentice-Hall, 1963.

O'Meara, T. *Thomas Aquinas, Theologian*. Notre Dame, IN: University of Notre Dame Press, 1997.

Orend, B. *The Morality of War*. Peterborough: Broadview Press, 2006.

Osborne, T. M. '*Divine Providence*: Thomist Premotion and Contemporary Philosophy of Religion'. *Nova et Vetera* 4 (2006): 607–631.

—*Love of Self and Love of God in Thirteenth Century Ethics*. Notre Dame, IN: University of Notre Dame Press, 2007.

—'Augustine and Aquinas on Foreknowledge Through Causes'. *Nova et Vetera* 6 (2008): 219–232.

—'The Threefold Referral of Acts to the Ultimate End in Thomas Aquinas and His Commentators'. *Angelicum* 85 (2008): 715–736.

Osler, M. J. *Divine Will and Mechanical Philosophy: Gassendi and Descartes on Contingency and Necessity in the Created World*. Cambridge: Cambridge University Press, 1994.

—'Whose Ends? Teleology in Early Modern Natural Philosophy'. *Osiris* 16 (2001): 151–168.

Owens, J. *The Doctrine of Being in the Aristotelian Metaphysics*. Toronto: Pontifical Institute of Mediaeval Studies, 1951.

—*St. Thomas Aquinas on the Existence of God: The Collected Papers of Joseph Owens*. Ed. J. Catan. Albany, NY: State University of New York Press, 1980.

—*Cognition: An Epistemological Inquiry*. Houston: Center for Thomistic Studies, 1992.

Panaccio, C. 'Aquinas on Intellectual Representation'. In *Ancient and Medieval Theories of Intentionality*. Ed. D. Perler, 185–202. Leiden: Brill, 2001.

Pasnau, R. *Theories of Cognition in the Later Middle Ages*. Cambridge: Cambridge University Press, 1997.

—*Thomas Aquinas on Human Nature: A Philosophical Study of 'Summa theologiae' Ia 75 –89*. Cambridge: Cambridge University Press, 2002.

Pasnau, R. and Shields, C. *The Philosophy of Aquinas*. Boulder, CO: Westview, 2004.

Pegis, A. C. 'The Separated Soul and its Nature in St. Thomas'. In *St. Thomas Aquinas, 1274–1974: Commemorative Studies*. 2 vols. 2: 131–158. Toronto: Pontifical Institute of Mediaeval Studies, 1974.

—*St. Thomas and the Problem of the Soul in the Thirteenth Century*. Reprint edition. Toronto: Pontifical Institute of Mediaeval Studies, 1978.

Pilsner, J. *Specification of Human Actions in St. Thomas Aquinas*. Oxford: Oxford University Press, 2006.

Pope, S. J., ed. *The Ethics of Aquinas*. Washington, DC: Georgetown University Press, 2002.

Porter, J. *The Recovery of Virtue: The Relevance of Aquinas for Christian Ethics*. Westminster: John Knox Press, 1990.

—'Virtue and Sin: The Connection of the Virtues and the Case of the Flawed Saint'. *The Journal of Religion* 75 (1995): 521–539.

—'What the Wise Person Knows: Natural Law and Virtue in Aquinas's *Summa Theologiae*'. *Studies in Christian Ethics* 1999: 57–69.

—'Virtue Ethics'. In *The Cambridge Companion to Christian Ethics*. Ed. R. Gill. Cambridge: Cambridge University Press, 2003.

—*Nature As Reason: A Thomistic Theory of the Natural Law*. Grand Rapids: W. B. Eerdmans Publishing Company, 2004.

Prado, C. G. 'The Third Way Revisited'. *New Scholasticism* 45 (1971): 495–501.

Quinn, J. 'The Third Way to God: A New Approach'. *The Thomist* 42 (1978): 50–68.

Rawls, J. *A Theory of Justice*. Cambridge, MA: Harvard University Press, 1971.

Raz, J. *The Morality of Freedom*. Oxford: Clarendon Press, 1986.

Reilly, J. *Saint Thomas on Law*. Toronto: Pontifical Institute of Mediaeval Studies, 1990.

Rhonheimer, M. *Natural Law and Practical Reason: A Thomist View of Moral Autonomy*. New York: Fordham University Press, 2000.

Rocca, G. *Speaking the Incomprehensible God: Thomas Aquinas on the Interplay of Positive and Negative Theology*. Washington, DC: Catholic University of America Press, 2004.

Rosemann, P. W. *Omne Agens Agit Sibi Simile*. Leuven: Leuven University Press, 1997.

Sedley, D. 'Is Aristotle's Teleology Anthropocentric?' *Phronesis* 36 (1991): 179–196.

Sherwin, M. S. *By Knowledge and By Love: Charity and Knowledge in the Moral Theology of St. Thomas Aquinas*. Washington, DC: Catholic University of America Press, 2005.

Sigmund, P. 'Law and Politics'. In *The Cambridge Companion to Aquinas*. Ed. N. Kretzmann and E. Stump, 217–231. Cambridge: Cambridge University Press, 1993.

Sorabji, R. *Time, Creation, and the Continuum: Theories in Antiquity and the Early Middle Ages*. Ithaca, NY: Cornell University Press, 1983.

Stark, R. *The Victory of Reason: How Christianity Led to Freedom, Capitalism, and Western Success*. New York: Random House, 2005.

Still, C. N. '"Gifted Knowledge": An Exception to Thomistic Epistemology?' *The Thomist* 63 2 (1999): 173–190.

—'Thomas Aquinas on the Assent of Faith'. In *Essays in Medieval Philosophy and Theology in Memory of Walter H. Principe, CSB*. Ed. J. R. Ginther and C. N. Still, 121–133. Aldershot: Ashgate, 2005.

Stump, E. *Aquinas*. London: Routledge, 2005.

Sweeney, L. 'Existence/Essence in Thomas Aquinas's Early Writings'. *Proceedings of the American Catholic Philosophical Association* 37 (1963): 97–131.

Sylla, E. D. 'Creation and Nature'. In *The Cambridge Companion to Medieval Philosophy*. Ed. A. S. McGrade, 171–195. Cambridge: Cambridge University Press, 2003.

Te Velde, R. *Participation and Substantiality in Thomas Aquinas*. Leiden and Boston: Brill, 1995.

Torrell, J.- P. *Aquinas's 'Summa': Background, Structure, and Reception*. Trans. B. M. Guevin. Washington, DC: Catholic University of America Press, 2005.

Van Nieuwenhove, R. and Wawrykow, J., eds. *The Theology of Thomas Aquinas*. Notre Dame, IN: University of Notre Dame Press, 2005.

Wallace, W. A. 'Newtonian Antinomies against the Prima Via'. *The Thomist* 19 (1956): 151–192.

—'The Cosmological Argument: A Reappraisal'. *Proceedings of the American Catholic Philosophical Association* 46 (1972): 43–57.

Walzer, M. *Just and Unjust Wars*. New York: Basic Books, 1977.

Wang, S. 'Aquinas on Human Happiness and the Natural Desire for God'. *New Blackfriars* 88 (2007): 322–334.

Weisheipl, J. 'Classification of the Sciences in Medieval Thought'. *Mediaeval Studies* 27 (1965): 54–90.

—'Quidquid movetur ab alio movetur: A Reply'. *New Scholasticism* 42 (1968): 422–431.

Weithman, P. 'Augustine and Aquinas on Original Sin and the Function of Political Authority'. *Journal of the History of Philosophy* 30 (1992): 353–376.

Wippel, J. F. 'Essence and Existence'. In *The Cambridge History of Later Medieval Philosophy*. Ed. N. Kretzmann, A. Kenny and J. Pinborg., 385–410. Cambridge: Cambridge University Press, 1982.

—*The Metaphysics of Thomas Aquinas: From Finite Being to Uncreated Being*. Washington, DC: Catholic University of America Press, 2000.

Wolfe, C. *Natural Law Liberalism*. Cambridge: Cambridge University Press, 2006.

Zuckert, M. 'The Fullness of Being: Thomas Aquinas and the Modern Critique of Natural Law'. *The Review of Politics* 69 (2007): 28–47.

INDEX

abstract thought 13, 22, 27–8,
    63, 95
abstraction 11, 30, 41, 54–9, 63
accidents (modifiers) 29–32, 52, 58,
    60–1, 73
    as unique 39, 48
acts: human 22, 45, 67, 70, 73, 76,
    78, 80, 86, 97
actuality
    see under potentiality
agnosticism 16, 57
Albert the Great 3
analogy (*analogia*) 3, 23–7, 65–6,
    70, 104–6
angels 31, 48–9, 64
    as immaterial 41, 57, 62–3
anima
    see soul
animals 67, 69, 81, 87, 94, 95
    humans as distinct from 39–40,
    42, 67, 68, 94–5
    'rational' 35, 61, 64, 77
    souls of 34, 40
Anselm 17–19
anti-perfectionism 102, 103
anti-social behaviours 77, 81, 85,
    96–7, 102
appetite 86, 89, 91, 105–6
    rational, *see* will
    sensory 11, 87, 89–90, *see also*
    desire
Aquinas, Thomas: as Christian
    theologian 1, 2, 4–8, 46, 109
    life of 3–5

Aristotle 4–8, 14, 28, 82–3
    Aquinas influenced by 3, 7–8, 12,
    19–20, 43, 51, 52, 54, 56–60,
    67, 70, 87–8, 90, 92, 93
    and metaphysics 28, 31–2, 33
    Metaphysics 14, 21
    Nicomachean Ethics 75
    On the Soul 41
    Politics 93, 104
    Posterior Analytics 59
    on science 11–13
    on the soul 34, 35, 37, 41–2,
    47–8, 57, 62
    on the state 94–5, 100, 108–9
atheism 16, 18–19
Augustine 2, 51, 110, 114
    on human beings 72, 96–7
    on politics 96
    on virtues 87
Averroes (Ibn Rushd) 5
Avicenna (Ibn Sīnā) 20–1, 28, 32

beatific vision 66, 73–4, 84, 87, 92
beatitude (*beatitudo*) 3, 49–50
    as distinct from happiness 70–1
    see also happiness
behaviour: purposeful 22, 67,
    69–70, 84
being (*ens*) 2, 11, 12, 14–22, 28–33,
    48–9, 63–6, 73–4, 79
    analogy of 23–6
    immaterial, *which see*
    see also angels, God, human beings
biology 11

faculties 41, 53, 87
faith (*fides*) 1–2, 16, 67, 87–8, 92
 Anselm on 17–19
 and reason 4, 5–8, 15–16, 46, 65–6
 fallibility 6, 23, 60, 61, 82
felicitas 3, 127n20, 131n81 *see*
 happiness
fideism 16–17
final cause 12, 13, 16, 60, 64,
 69–70
first cause 11, 14, 23, 65, 73
"five ways" (*quinque viae*) 4, 19–22,
 23, 64
form 12–13, 24–33, 37–40, 42–3,
 50, 55–6, 59–60
 sensible 53, 61, 65
 subsistent 35, 46–8, 62
 substantial 28–32, 35, 46–8
formal cause 12–13, 23, 60
 see also quiddity
freedom of choice (*liberum
 arbitrium*) 67–8, 78–9

Ghandi 112
Gilson, Etienne 2
God: essence of (divine) 16–17,
 23–5, 27, 64–6, 73
 as first cause 11, 14, 23, 73
 goodness of 16, 24–7, 45, 64, 72
 as ground of being 11, 14–15, 33
 as immaterial 2–3, 40, *see also*
 immaterial beings
 as necessary being 23, 33, 64, 70
 as omnipotent 15–16, 78
 as prime mover 7, 19–20, 70
 as self-subsistent being
 (*ipsum esse subsistens*) 15, 23
 study of 11–22, 23–4, 26–7
good, the 22, 69, 71–2, 74, 76, 77,
 78–81, 84–5, 89
 common, *which see*
 as natural object of the will 44–5
 pursuit of 79–81, 87, 97, 98

government 93, 96–101, 111
grace 65
Grotius, Hugo 112

habit 82, 83, 86, 87, 114
 and children 101–2
 synderesis 79
happiness 2, 67–74, 77, 87–8, 89,
 103–4, 105, 106
 as ultimate destiny of human
 beings 3, 4, 7, 49, 70–2, 78–9,
 80–4, 92, 105
health 26, 72
Heraclitus 75
hierarchy of being 63–4
Hobbes, Thomas 111, 113
honour 71–2
hope (*spes*) 87, 92
human beings: as distinct from
 animals 39–40, 42, 67, 68, 94–5
 participation in God 23, 27, 40,
 69, 72, 74
 as unity of soul and body, *which see*
human good 27, 99
human law (*lex humana*) 75, 83–4,
 101–9
hylomorphic: beings 29–30, 32,
 distinction 31

Ibn Rushd (Averroes) 5
Ibn Sīnā (Avicenna) 20–1, 28, 32
images 48, 57, 65
imagination 18, 30, 56, 65
immaterial: beings 5, 30, 35, 40, 57,
 62–3
 intellect as 5, 42, 43, 52
 knowledge of 43, 62
immortality 2, 5, 35, 45–50, 61
 incorruptibility of the human
 soul 40, 46–8
intellect 4, 17, 23, 28, 35, 40–4, 48,
 53–5, 64–6, 72–4, 79, 90
 as active or passive 42–4